Paradigm Lost, Paradigm Regained:
The Worldview of Ali A. Mazrui

Paradigm Lost, Paradigm Regained: The Worldview of Ali A. Mazrui

By
Seifudein Adem

Global Humanities Press
Provo, Utah
2002

Copyright © 2002 by Global Humanities Press
All rights reserved. No portion of this publication may be dupl- icated in any way without the expressed written consent of the publisher, except in the form of brief excerpts or quotations for review purposes.

Library of Congress Cataloging-in-Publication Data

Seifudein Adem, *Paradigm Lost, Paradigm Regained*

ISBN 0-9724918-3-X

Published by Global Humanities Press
Brigham Young Unviersity, Provo, Utah
Distributed by Global Scholarly Publications
220 Madison Avenue
New York, New York 10016
Phone: (212) 679-6410   Fax: (212) 679-6424
E-mail: books@gsp-online.org
www.gsp-online.org

Acknowledgements

Most of the research work for this book was done when I was at first an assistant professor and then a Foreign Scholar at the Institute of Social Sciences, University of Tsukuba, Japan, between April 2000 and March 2003. I am grateful for the institutional affiliation and for various forms of support.

A substantial part of the final phase of the work was completed in the summer months of 2002 when I was a Research Associate at the Institute of Global Cultural Studies at the State University of New York in Binghamton. I am grateful for this opportunity and for the financial assistance from the Research Foundation of State University of New York.

In Binghamton I received various forms of support from several individuals. Professor Ali A. Mazrui, the Director of the Institute and the man behind the ideas I discuss in the book, granted me extensive interviews during the limited intervals he had between his domestic and international lecture tours. Reading Mazrui's books is in many ways like conversing with him (there will be more about that later in this book). However, to be able to sit face-to-face and converse one-on-one with the man himself, who has a pleasant face, a gifted tongue, and a wise mind, was quite an exhilarating and learning experience for me. I am more grateful for these conversations than I can say.

I am indebted also to Ruzima C. Sebuharara, and Robert Ostergaurd, as well as to Nancy Levis, Goretti Mugambwa, Barbara Tierno, and Anna Maria Palombaro, for their patient and helpful counsel. Special thanks is due to A. S. Bemath, the Mazruiana bibliographer. His book on Mazruiana, and my own personal correspondence with him, was very instrumental in facilitating the preparation of the manuscript for this book. Last, and most of all, I thank my wife, Kayoko, who assisted me with technical matters in addition to making me feel at home during our stay in New York; and Nina, our daughter, who always cheered us up in her own way, and often kept us enjoyably busy.

Once again, I extend my sincere appreciation to the institutions and individuals mentioned above and to those that are left out of the list. Any flaws, errors, or contestable opinions in this book are, of course, the responsibility of only the author.

Table of Contents

Foreword
Preface

1. Introduction 1
   Mazruiana: Essence and Genesis 1
   Logic of Reasoning in Mazruiana 3
   Mazruiana's Theory of Knowledge 5
   Notes 7

2. Ali A. Mazrui and the Study of IR 9
   Introduction 9
   Mazruiana and Its Critics: Part I 15
   Mazruiana and Its Critics: Part II 18
   Conclusion 21
   Notes 25

3. Mazruiana and the New International Relations 29
   Introduction 29
   The Social Constructivism of Mazruiana 30
   Mazruiana on the Nature of Contemporary
       International System 35
   Conclusion 50
   Notes 53

4. Mazruiana Epistemology and Style 57
   Introduction 57
   Why Mazrui Writes 57
   Semi-Autobiographical Style 62
   Styles of Argument 63
   Notes 75

5. Culture and Development in Mazruiana Pedagogy:
   Africa and Japan Compared ... 77
   Introduction ... 77
   Explaining the Japanese Miracle ... 78
   Flexibility in Japanese Culture ... 82
   The African Condition: A Mazruiana Diagnosis ... 84
   Mazruiana and the New Culturalism ... 88
   Learning How to learn ... 91
   Conclusion ... 94
   Notes ... 94

6. Between Social Theory and Public Policy:
   Mazruiana in Application ... 99
   Introduction ... 99
   A Paradigm Shift? ... 104
   The End of the End of History ... 107
   The Invention of the Clash of Civilizations ... 110
   The Discourse of Clashism ... 117
   From Democratic Peace to Theocratic Peace? ... 125
   Conclusion ... 129
   Notes ... 130

7. Ideas in Words ... 135
   Introduction ... 135
   A Mazruiana Glossary ... 135
   Notes ... 175

8. Paradigm Lost, Paradigm regained:
   A Conclusion ... 179
   Notes ... 186

Appendix ... 187
Bibliography ... 193
Index

Foreword

It may be odd for someone who is neither a scholar of African studies nor a specialist on Ali Mazrui's works (or Mazruiana) to write a foreword to this interesting piece of work by Seifudein Adem. However, even for a person not adequately informed about the subject, this book provides a well-structured and coherently organized review of the works and ideas of Ali Mazrui. The book renders a systematic account of Mazruiana, a task which is by no means easy given especially the eclectic nature of the works.

In addition, the complexity of Mazruiana is compounded by the unique epistemological orientation which it utilizes to tackle a wide variety of social scientific issues. But, above all, Mazrui's critical perspective towards the hegemonic and hierarchical structure of international power and intellectual relations is perhaps why Mazruiana is "systematically ignored in the academic discipline." (I must admit, I am one of those IR students who are so integrated to the system that ignored Mazruiana). In any case, this book dissects and scrutinizes Mazruiana in terms of its methodology, critics, theory and style. I will be surprised, therefore, if the book does not prove to be not only an excellent guide to the worldview of Ali Mazrui but also an important contribution to the critique of the existing theories of international relations (IR).

The theory and practice of IR, at the time of writing, is quite worrisome. The US administration is progressively shifting its gear towards a neoconservative route, and its unilateral approach seems to be insulated from any form of serious criticism. It is almost indubitable that Huntington's *Clash of Civilization* and the neorealist epistemological frame underpin the idea and logic of the policies of the Bush administration. As Chapter 5 of this book rightfully argues, Mazruiana interrogates such contemporary issues as well and offers an alternative way of viewing the world systems. It is my honest hope that this book would in this regard induce and stimulate debate in the academic and political world.

As it stands, the major contribution of this book may be in its successful attempt to situate Mazruiana's position in the academic discipline of international relations. Seifudein Adem, who lives in and is associated with Japanese society, is a promising African IR scholar. Adem's journey from Africa to Japan corresponds to the one Mazrui's embarked on earlier. But their respective journeys took them to different, and some might even say opposite, destinations. However that may be, Adem's experience in Japan has sharpened his perspective by placing him in unique angle to challenge the Eurocentric intellectual hegemony. In this sense, it can be said, Mazrui and Adem form a counter-hegemonic coalition through this book.

Adem indicates in the concluding chapter that the works of Mazrui share certain crucial features with that of Ibn Khaldun, the source of inspirations for many postmodernist IR theories. Since Robert Cox advocated the relevancy of Ibn Khaldun many years ago, the idea of *posthegemonic order* has become one of the academic attractions and inspirations for IR scholars. If Cox's work could in this way provoke discussion in the academic field, there is no reason why Adem's work—which is of the same genre--would not do likewise.

October 2002
Kazuto Suzuki
College of International Studies,
University of Tsukuba

Preface

Perhaps there are two factors that influence which scholarly works we choose to read. One is based on the popularity (or 'the noise factor') pertaining to the works. We may not concur with the scholar's philosophy, and we may not even fully understand his/her ideas, but in order to keep abreast of the state of the discipline, we decide to read some works. On the other hand, we may choose to read a particular author because of our fascination with the writer's ideas -- their originality, clarity, and philosophy, or any combination of these. I admit from the outset that the second factor featured most prominently in my decision to continue to read Ali Mazrui, from the time I was able to put my hand on his published works. While reading Mazrui's works, one can enjoy his unique qualities of presentation, and at the same time keep abreast of significant global events. A reader, of course, always reserves the right not to buy into some of Mazrui's conclusions, but one thing is clear; to read Mazrui's writings, and to listen to his lectures, means to know more, while getting the utmost pleasure from the process of knowing itself.

The inspiration to write this book comes from my longstanding doubt about the adequacy of the attention paid to the works of Ali A. Mazrui. This is not to imply that Mazrui has not already reached a pinnacle of fame; he has indeed. However, I contend that the value of the works of Mazrui go far beyond the recognition they have achieved thus far. The strong desire to look into the works more systematically is also part and parcel of the factors that influenced the inception of this book project.

Because of the restrictions imposed upon me by my field of training, I focus in this book mainly on the political science aspects of the works of Ali Mazrui. However, there is no doubt in my mind that other scholars would also approach and analyze his works from the perspectives of history, and philosophy, as well as other related fields. Fortunately, encouraging signs are already visible in this regard.

This book is structured as follows. In chapter one I focus on "the second-order" issues relating to the foundational units of the works of Ali Mazrui – namely, the epistemology and theory of knowledge, as well as the logic of reasoning. This chapter is intended to provide a framework for contextualizing the discussion in the rest of the book.

In the second chapter I start out with a preliminary substantiation of my contention that although Mazrui has already reached a pinnacle of fame, his works have not been fully utilized. Then I grapple with the question of why Ali Mazrui's works might have been marginalized, by looking briefly at both the substantive features and the scope of his works, against the background of the criticism directed at them.

In the third chapter, I take the discussion further by demonstrating why Mazrui's works could be regarded as a seminal contribution to what I call the new International Relations. Since a good deal of Mazrui's writings grapple with substantive or "first-order" issues, I aspire in this chapter to interpretively analyze some of them, and articulate my assessment of where they fit in the academic discourse, and why.

Chapter four moves away from the substance to the form of the works of Ali Mazrui. My principal purpose here is to shed light on the technical aspects of the works of Ali Mazrui, especially in respect to epistemology and style. Chapter five, which is a later insertion into the book, examines the teachings of Mazruiana on the relationship between culture and development.

In chapter six I apply Mazruiana methodology as well as its concepts to the analysis of a contemporary issue in world politics, with an intention to demonstrate the usefulness of closely studying the multifaceted works of Ali Mazrui, both as a method and epistemology of social research. It must be understood that while some of the organizing concepts and the methodological framework are borrowed from the works of Ali Mazrui, the arguments and the conclusions in this chapter are those of the author, and may not necessarily be shared by Ali Mazrui.

Towards the end of the book comes a chapter, *Ideas in Words*, which, although a glossary, should be read as more than an ordinary collection of words. It contains a summary of some of Mazrui's neologisms, though it is not by any means exhaustive, and also contains familiar words, combined or formulated by him in unfamiliar ways. The chapter is written with the convenience of the reader in mind—a consideration reflected in two ways.

First, although I am aware from Mazrui's own references and notes that a handful of the words were coined by other people and had been used here and there before he used them, the context of Mazrui's usage of them is totally different, and almost unique, so as to make them an integral part of a discussion of the works of Ali Mazrui. Therefore, in those few instances I have decided not to bother myself (and the reader) with documenting the sources.

Secondly, since part of the reason for including such a chapter is to demonstrate Mazrui's capacity to coin words that are new or that are combined in new ways with meanings that are at once concise, deep and comprehensive, I have tried for the most part to keep intact Mazrui's own inimitable definitions. In a few other cases, I have tried to adapt those definitions or allusions to the meaning. In both cases, convention requires that I use quotation marks where Mazrui's exact words are used, but considering that a strict adherence to this rule would significantly disrupt the flow of reading, I have dispensed with the marks in most cases. However, for cross-reference, and further reading, as well as for reasons of acknowledgment, I have given bibliographical details of the source material. It is my hope that this chapter, *Ideas in Words*, will provide useful tools for taxonomic analysis in a wide field of inquiries. For those interested in it, it also offers a conceptual framework that is less burdened with Eurocentric bias. This is *not* of course to suggest that the concepts assembled in this chapter are neutral or innocent; they are far from it. These concepts openly expose and challenge the inadequacy of the prevailing 'regime of truth,' and offer an alternative that is informed by a non-Western worldview. They expose the bias in the predominant discursive formation. The Eurocentric bias in the production and re-production of knowledge is divulged with these concepts, with the skillful use of a tradition of analysis, which was itself constructed in Europe. It appears that Mazrui has taken to heart that old African proverb, "One can pluck out the thorn from the flesh with a thorn."

The title of the concluding chapter is also the title of this book, *Paradigm Lost, Paradigm Regained*. From a comparative perspective, this chapter briefly demonstrates how Mazruiana fulfilled Ibn Khaldun's paradigmic aspiration. The conclusion of this concluding chapter, and therefore of this book, says that through a closer study of the worldview of Ali A. Mazrui, we might be able to *regain the lost paradigm of Ibn Khaldun*, in its reinvigorated and postmodern form.

All in all, the materials consulted cover most of the works of Ali A. Mazrui, from his early writings to the most recent ones, but the study in the book is thematic, and not chronological.

Ali Mazrui is not only the most distinguished writer to have emerged from independent Black Africa, and the most penetrating and discriminating expositor of the ideology of the Third World, but he is also a most illuminating interpreter of the drift of world politics….The issues that interest him, the audience to whom he addresses himself, even the values he embraces, are not simply black or African or Third World, but global.

(Hedley Bull, 1978)

1. Introduction

Mazruiana: Essence and Genesis

Ontologically, a body of knowledge can be defined in at least two ways. One is through delineating its boundaries by specifying where it fits within the established disciplinary domains. In this sense, Mazruiana, and hereafter this is the term I shall use most often, refers to the multifaceted works of Ali Mazrui in the fields of international relations, comparative politics, political theory and philosophy, sociology, sociolinguistics and literary studies. This was how the late Omari Kokole used the term, and I shall stick in this book to the same usage.[1]

The second ontological way of defining a body of knowledge can be in terms of its subject matter. In its entirety, this book is an attempt to define Mazruiana in a substantive sense. Yet it is still possible, and perhaps even indispensable, to supply here a working definition of Mazruiana in the above sense. Mazruiana is a body of interdisciplinary knowledge that focuses on the comparative study of the role of culture in global affairs, with emphasis on language and identity both as subjects of analysis and tools of deconstruction. It is also an approach for acquiring such knowledge.

Mazruiana in the second sense represents a self-contained body of knowledge, with its own notion of the criteria for acquiring a valid knowledge and its own unique logic of reasoning. It also has its own unique style and its own building blocks or concepts—these are discussed in chapters four and six respectively. What emerges from all of the above is a useful framework of analysis that is anchored in certain core epistemological and methodological assumptions. This is not, of course, to suggest that ontological and epistemological levels in academic discourse are always separable from or independent of one another. This Mazruiana framework is applied in chapter five to demonstrate how it can be utilized for grappling with contemporary global issues.

On the other hand, this introductory chapter concerns itself mainly with the issues surrounding the methodology as well as the logic of reasoning in Mazruiana. It is hard to precisely trace all of the factors that have contributed to the evolution and development of Mazruiana. Yet it can be said that both nurture and nature have played a part. The origin of Mazrui's interest in political science, which is also the focal point of this book, is far less obscure. In an autobiographical passage in *The Making of an African Political Scientist*, Mazrui attributed his attraction to political discourse to "a childhood interest in law and journalism" and to his "family background."[2]

Some of Mazrui's ideas, as his philosophy of knowledge, are therefore products of the influence of his upbringing and environment. Mazrui himself recounts that his idea of social distance as a precondition for political legitimacy, as well as his general concern with problems of culture and violence, are traceable to a 'little incident' in which he had taken part in Zanzibar, when he was only six. The incident involved Mazrui, and another little boy who had intruded in Mazrui's playground only to be chased away later. The 'little incident' assumed greater significance moments later with the involvement of parents on both sides. This incident was later to inform Mazrui's perspective on the tension between the group of Swahilized Arabs, who were Mazrui's hosts, and the group of Arabized Swahilis of Zanzibar, to which the "other" little boy belonged.[3] Mazrui's reflection on this incident is indeed an indication that he has an observant, precise mind, that has a great capacity for abstraction. Even if many of us encounter such an experience in one form or another, certainly not many of us would think of it in these terms, and far fewer of us would use this "data" for critically interrogating remotely similar situations at the macro level, as Mazrui was to do later on in his life. What needs also to be noted is that in his account of the incident and how it later influenced his thought, Mazrui did not claim that the ideas he later put into use were "revealed" to him in his childhood. Instead he acknowledged that at the time he had not sufficiently understood what the incident meant.

Similarly, Mazrui gives account of another lesson acquired from an apparently ordinary experience while he was a teenager working as a junior clerk at the Mombassa Institute of Muslim Education. That was when a shorts-wearing European reminded him that it was improper to wear pajama pants in a school's dining hall. This, Mazrui tells, was for him another "lesson in culture conflict."[4] The genesis of Mazruiana methodology, its thematic concerns and epistemological orientation, may be traceable to such formative experiences.

Logic of Reasoning in Mazruiana

The whole accounts of the incidents above, and the more systematic thoughts Mazrui articulated later on in his life, together with an explanation of how the former came to influence his general perspective, beg an important question of the logic of reasoning in Mazruiana. Is Mazruiana to be understood as a deductivist or inductivist body of knowledge? As I shall elaborate later, it appears that a substantial part of Mazruiana is based on deductivism, but to the extent that Mazruiana's generalizations are based, such as in the above stories and in his many others works, on prior specific observations, it is also possible to interpret Mazruiana as an inductively informed body of knowledge. Moreover, in view of Mazruiana's emphasis on and even advocacy for the usage of autobiography as a source of political data - a subject to which I shall return later in the book - it can be said that inductivism also provides a methodological basis for Mazruiana.

However, on closer examination, it appears that the evidence for a deductivist and an inductivist interpretation of Mazruiana is even. Still, a question persists: in spite of this fact, or because of it, where would we situate Mazruiana along a methodological plane? Is there a unity between Mazruiana's inductivism and its deductivism? The tentative answer I wish to offer in relation to the second question, which hopefully also answers the first one, if only partially, is that Mazruiana surpasses the rigid, conventional division between inductivism and deductivism. This, in effect, also amounts to an implicit rejection of the separation between the "imaginative" and the "real" world, firmly basing itself on an anti-essentialist ontological foundation. Perhaps behind all this is something akin to what Karl Popper, quoting Albert Einstein, once referred to as intuition based upon something like an intellectual love (*Einfuhlung*) of the objects of experience.[5] *Einfuhlung* and Mazruiana's methodological inclination, as described above, appear to be substantially compatible. In its commitment, Mazruiana is empirical, but not empiricist. Its generalizations are based on empirical observations, but it does not assume that there is a one-to-one correspondence between the "reality" we observe and the object of observation as it exists. What is observed in a mirror is sometimes more real than the object it reflects. This subject is further explored in chapter three.

In terms of style, it is impossible to read more than a few lines of a piece of writing by Mazrui without knowing that it was written by him. One reason for this is that he writes in a direct, and not a roundabout way. Another reason is the unique form of Mazruiana; its powerfully insightful usage of comparative antithesis in its arguments. This theme shall be treated more fully in chapter four of the book. For now, it suffices to say that Mazruiana often compares what is almost always incomparable at first glance. Almost every time one comes across a Mazruiana comparison, the immediate reaction will be, "what do these two (events, people, processes etc) have in common?" Now, the question arises, what does it take to develop such a high level of sharpness and sophistication in making penetrating comparative analyses? Such investigative reasoning certainly requires, among other things, a deep empirical knowledge of and an intimate familiarity with subjects across a broad spectrum of fields, along with the capacity to critically analyze and synthesize it. In addition, what is required for undertaking an insightful comparative analyses is a knowledge that is acquired not merely through the outer five sense but, and most significantly, a knowledge acquired through what John Locke called *reflection*, a form of knowledge acquired through inner senses.[6] I shall take up this subject again in chapters two and four.

Mazruiana's Theory of Knowledge

Mazrui has stated that one aspect of his theory refers to how knowledge can be acquired or enriched. This was in one of his very early writings, *Edmund Burke and Reflections on the Revolution in the Congo*, from which a the following, rather long quotation is worthwhile:

> There are at least five ways of treating a political theory. One is to consider it a form of intellectual exercise, pure and simple—an adventure in abstraction to sharpen the mind. Another is to get through it, and through other theories, seeking a personal political theory for oneself. A third is to distill the history out of a political theory— examine what light the theory can throw on the age from which it emerged. A fourth is also to treat the theory as a source of historical

data, but not in the sense in which a river may conceivably be a source of some dissolved substance from the silt it carries, but in the sense in which a river may be a source of water. In this latter sense a political theory is not distilled to yield history. It is itself part of the flow of history—part of what Americans sometimes call intellectual history. A fifth way may involve tearing the theory out of its historical context altogether, and bringing the logic of all or some of its ideas to bear on a specific situation in perhaps one's own time—the object of the exercise being to determine whether the ideas scattered within the theory help in the understanding of the situation, on the one hand, and on the other, whether the situation can lend a new depth to the theory or perhaps expose an old shallowness within it. For those who are called upon to teach European political theory to students outside Europe, this last approach may often be particularly profitable. The 'Europeanism' of the theory is thus played down as the ideas are pulled out of their temporal and geographical context and analyzed for what they may have to say about some situation, say, Asia or Africa at the present time...There is always the possibility that it may produce nothing new, but the cross breeding is worth attempting all the time.[7]

The first of the above approaches is unitary and theoretical, the second is multiple and applied, the third is a socio-historical approach, and the fourth is called a historical approach. The fifth is perhaps the most innovative approach, and may well be called the Mazruiana approach. This is, of course, not to imply that the traces of each of the remaining four approaches are absent in Mazruiana. Instead it is to suggest that it is the fifth one that animates most of the works of Ali Mazrui. Almost in all of his works Mazrui elegantly and quite productively employs this approach of "tearing the theory out of its historical context altogether [and the history out of its theoretical context], and bringing the logic of all or some of its ideas to bear on a specific situation in [one's] own time."[8] In most of his works this approach is explicit, and in a few others it is less so, but it is almost always there.

One of the works in which the usage of this approach is most straightforward is *Thoughts on Assassination in Africa*.⁹ In this work, Mazrui advanced a hypothesis on political assassinations in Africa by drawing on the philosophical ideas of Jean Bodin and Montesquieu, the 16th and the 18th century French political philosophers, respectively. What Mazrui was engaged in doing in that piece was, in effect, "tearing a theory out of its historical context" and using it to further our understanding of a significant political phenomenon in his own time. This was, in turn, an application of a methodology laid out in another of Mazrui's works, *Political Science and Political Futurology*.¹⁰

Epistemologically, the five approaches listed above are deductivist. Thus, if we view them in conjunction with the aforementioned story of the 'little incident' and how it came to influence Mazrui's paradigm later, it becomes clear how inductivism and deductivism are fused into one in Mazruiana. One conclusion that can be drawn from this is that for Mazruiana "reality," both in theory and in fact, is wrapped in the complementariness of the interaction between opposites. And no wonder then, that paradox occupies such a central place in Mazruiana's style of scientific investigation, a topic discussed more fully in chapter four.

1 Kokole (1998a: xxi-xxii).
2 Mazrui (1973a: 102).
3 Mazrui (1973a: 109).
4 Mazrui (1986a: 34); for further discussion see Mazrui (1987c: 217).
5 Popper (1968: 32).
6 Locke (1997: 120-122).
7 Mazrui (1963a:122).
8 Mazrui (1963a:122).
9 Mazrui (1968b: 40-58).
10 Mazrui (1969c: 172-188).

2. Ali A. Mazrui and the Study of IR

Introduction

In the twentieth century, Ali Mazrui reached a pinnacle of fame as one of *the* leading intellectual figures of our time. He also attained at the same time *de facto* recognition as an eminent scholar of International Relations (IR). This fame and recognition is evident from the acclamation he has received and continues to receive (See Appendix). In fact, his recognition goes back to 1964 when he published an award-winning essay in *International Organization*.[1] Now Mazrui has under his name more than twenty books and over 400 major academic articles, and many of these were published in highly acclaimed journals of political science and international relations.[2]

Yet it is fair to contend that the formal credit accorded to Mazruiana in IR pales when compared to his immense contribution. What I am suggesting here is, in other words, Mazruiana has been systematically ignored in the academic discipline. Whether or not Mazrui considers himself an IR scholar rather than say, a scholar of comparative politics,[3] the first question I am inclined to ask is: why the imbalance?

In order to offer a tentative answer one would perhaps necessarily have to look first at Mazruiana's hallmark: eclecticism. Mazrui's works - embracing as they do a rich epistemic terrain - could not *readily* be pigeonholed into any one of the predominant schools in IR. In the broadness of its scope, in the diversity of the area it covers and, above all, in its basic assumptions and propositions, it can be argued, however, that Mazruiana has a close affinity with the social constructivist school in IR. I shall return to this theme in chapter three. Some analysts have also, in any case, attempted to situate Mazruiana within the broader IR discipline.

In a commendably original work, for instance, John Harbeson sought to conduct 'a macro-level inquiry' into Mazruiana in the context of contemporary thought in the IR. In that work, Harbeson referred to the works of well-known IR scholars such as Hans Morganthau, Joseph Nye, and Kenneth Waltz with a view to relating elements of their theories to Mazruiana. Harbeson argued:

> An implicit and unstated hypothesis of Mazrui appears to be that the culture of politics is defined by those whose actions and pronouncements have the most profound and far-reaching impact on the sensibilities of a people or age; those who have exerted the most cultural power regardless of as to who views their impact as beneficent and who views it as malevolent. Indeed it may be that in this sense Mazrui fits more comfortably than might be apparent initially within the realist philosophical tradition reaching from Machiavelli to Morganthau. Culture is, as he says, about power, particularly the power of ideas.[4]

Harbeson's premise is correct, but his conclusion is not. Even a cursory reading of basic IR literature suggests that the line of thought that regards "culture as power, particularly the power of ideas" fits much more neatly in the social constructivist IR school than in the realist philosophical tradition. Without denying that Mazruiana does share some basic realist assumptions, such as the ultimate proclivity of

Paradigm Lost, Paradigm Regained 11

man (but not woman) towards war,[5] or what it calls elsewhere, "the masculinity of war,"[6] over all, realism is simply too materialistic and too realpolitik-centered to demonstrate affinity with Mazruiana. The normative commitment in Mazruiana seems to show abhorrence to the immoral fabric of the realist theory. As Harbeson himself correctly observed later in the same piece:

> Where Morganthau saw military and political power as being of primary importance, and cultural norms as secondary, Mazrui seems to do the reverse; power in human history emanates less out of the barrel of the gun than from the mouths of prophets, poets, playwrights, and philosophers.[7]

Describing Mazruiana in terms such as the used above is accurate. In fairness to Harbeson, it must also be pointed out that epistemologically, but only epistemologically, there is a sense that Mazruiana comes closer to the classical realist approach. The following is how Hedley Bull, himself an ardent follower of this school, defined the classical approach.

> the approach to theorizing that derives from philosophy, history, and law, and that is characterized above all by explicit reliance upon the exercise of judgment and by the assumptions that if we confine ourselves to strict standards of verification and proof there is very little of significance that can be said about international relations, that general propositions about this subject must therefore derive from a scientifically imperfect process of perception or intuition...[8]

Yet despite such epistemological affinity between Mazrui and the classical realists, the former uses concepts that are more operational and less abstract than the latter. I will return to this subject in chapter three. Alamin Mazrui's analysis of Mazruiana in respect to African languages also points to an obvious but a less remarked upon fact that Mazrui's arguments align with social constructivism.[9] True to its eclectic inclinations, Mazruiana also shares points of views with other schools in the IR. In addition to the assumption that man's nature is war prone, which Mazruiana shares with classical realism, it rejects, like neorealism, the idea that nuclear proliferation is necessarily inimical to global stability. Mazruiana's reasoning is nevertheless implicitly ethical, though it is also based on long-term security considerations, in contrast to neorealism's preoccupation only with the latter. In Mazrui's own words:

> Some degree of proliferation may shock the five principal nuclear powers out of their complacency. The proliferation would gradually convince them that this system of a few select nuclear powers cannot be long sustained. Therefore we should aim for global nuclear disarmament, universal renunciation of these evil weapons for everybody, not just for all but the five countries but for everybody.[10]

Mazrui articulated a more or less similar position in 1982, in a work titled *The Computer Culture and Nuclear Power*.[11] Prior to that he had argued in the same vein, stressing, "a dose of the disease becomes part of the necessary cure."[12] The ethical component in Mazrui's discourse is clearly implied in his discussion of what he called *nuclear apartheid*, "a situation where five Nuclear haves who are under no pressure to give up their own weapons of mass destruction, and many nuclear Have-Nots who are punished when they presume to go nuclear, or build arsenal of mass destruction."[13]

Like neoliberal institutionalism, Mazruiana places greater emphasis on the utility of institutions. Mazruiana's institutionalist position is articulated most systematically in the *World Culture and the Search for Human Consensus*.[14] I return to this subject in chapter three. Like feminism, Mazruiana stresses the role of woman in liberating humankind from the danger of war.[15] Sometimes Mazruiana also employs concepts that rhyme with the world-systems approach.[16] But the intersection between Mazruiana and these theories is not surprising since they are all animated by certain common assumptions, and are guided by generally similar normative and methodological orientations.[17]

Rather than being an approach that has imposed itself on Mazruiana, eclecticism is a mode of analysis with which Mazrui consciously and comfortably identifies himself. The kind of eclecticism which guides Mazruiana, as Mazrui states in *Eclecticism as an Ideological Alternative*, is "…creative eclecticism (implying a genius for selectivity, for synthesizing disparate elements, and for ultimate independent growth in the intellectual field)."[18] Mazrui's eclecticism therefore takes a variety of forms. He is an eclectic in the sense of being able to easily change gears between the role of an ideologue, an intellectual, a scholar and an artist.[19] His eclecticism also expresses itself in his interest in and contribution to diverse fields of inquiry. No wonder, Mazrui has been described variously as Scholar, Ideologue, Philosopher and Artist[20]; 'The Lawyer'[21], and Islamicisit;[22] and so forth. But in describing Mazruiana one should always be wary of the proverbial mistake of those visually challenged individuals who tried to describe an elephant merely on the basis of the part of it each was able to touch.

As hinted earlier, apart from disciplinary eclecticism, the other form of expression of Mazruiana's eclecticism is theoretical—and this is what I am primarily concerned with here. In a divided discipline such as IR, an eclectic scholar in this sense runs the risk of being written off as theoretically uninformed. That is to say that contemporary IR seems to place higher premium on allegiance to a particular worldview, although, it must be admitted, there are scholars in the field who are well recognized in spite of the difficulty of conveniently categorizing their works as belonging to this or that school of thought in the discipline. But these scholars are the exceptions that prove the rule. The odds are almost always against intellectuals who are reluctant to embrace the teachings of the "established theories," at least under most circumstances.

Side by side with the tendency of ignoring "unorthodox" works, another explanation for Mazruiana's relative obscurity in IR would seem to pertain to the predominance of the Anglo-Saxon, top-bottom view in the academic discipline. Mazrui is, in the words of a close observer, "an incisive critic of the *status quo* and a member of that same group at the same time."[23] Apart from membership, who and what type of issues are privileged by the *status quo* and who and what type of issues are not, is also a well-known fact. Ole Waever nearly recognized this fact when he pointed out referring to the exclusion of prominent non-Western thinkers from *The Future of International Relations: Masters in the Making?*, a book Waever co-authored in 1997, "that [if it had not been for] the relative dominance of Anglo-American IR…it would have been nice to have had a chapter on [Ali] Mazrui or [Takashi] Inoguchi."[24]

Perhaps an even more directly related factor than the preceding one is Mazrui's distaste for Zionism. On several occasions, such as in his *Cultural Forces in World Politics,* Mazrui dared to compare Zionism with apartheid.[25] This was obviously irritatingly unacceptable to most, if not all, of the followers of the Jewish faith. The question which arises is therefore whether or not Mazruiana's anti-Zionist proclivity has also contributed to its marginalization in the IR, given that many of the influential voices in the field are themselves mainly Jewish. Chaly Sawere's observation seems to support such a view: "Mazrui's open anti-Zionist advocacy has sometimes come into conflict with the more disguised pro-Zionist establishment of American academia."[26]

Despite his reluctance to cease saying and writing things that were likely to "hurt" the feelings of some Jewish intellectuals, Mazrui did nevertheless recognize that there could be personal and professional risks if his anti-Zionist pronouncements were misconstrued, as they probably were, as a reflection of anti-Semitism. In his *World Culture and the Black Experience,* a book based on his John Danz lecture delivered in 1974, he related such risks in quite concrete terms. In it he narrated the sorry fate of John Hatchett and James Turner, two black faculty members at New York and Cornell Universities respectively, who were dismissed for their anti-Semitic public statements.[27] Later on Mazrui articulated, in even clearer terms, the risks involved in not embracing Zionism, or at the very least, in not leaving it alone as if it were a sacred cow. In his own words, "[o]pposition to Zionism by a Jew was now interpreted as 'Jewish self-hate' and anti-Zionism in a gentile was interpreted as anti-Semitism."[28]

Although at times Mazrui's arguments seem to have anti-Zionist overtones, he has also often been straightforward in according a disproportionately high credit to Jewish intellectuals, when and where he thought that they were deserving. In the same work in which he related the story of John Hatchett and James Turner, he, for instance, unequivocally lauds the "amazing impact of the Jews on the history of ideas at large," and the "disproportionate contribution from the ideas of Jewish thinkers or Jewish prophets."

In a different but related context, Mazrui had sensed and lamented what he called the "paradox of the American condition"- - intolerance of non-mainstream ideas. Mazrui posed the question in his *Uncle Sam's Hearing Aid* in 1985: "Why is America an effective communicator but an inattentive listener?" He then suggested that the situation could be rectified through "...an enhanced American tolerance of global cultural pluralism."[29]

I should now like to turn to some of the more specific criticism directed against Mazruiana, and see if it can be cleared away.

Mazruiana and Its Critics: Part I

Understandably there will be those who do not buy into all or some of the preceding partial explanations for what appears to be a systematic disregard of Mazruiana in IR. The relative oversight of

Mazruiana in IR, some may argue, is due to the preoccupation of Mazruiana with issues relating to the Third World. However, at least two problems attend to this form of reasoning. First, Mazruiana does not only concern itself with Third World issues. In fact it is tempting to say, twisting around in part what Colin Leys once said about Mazrui's "incapability to write a dull paragraph,"[30] that Mazrui is incapable of restricting himself to a narrow field of inquiry. As indicated in the epigraph of this book, Hedley Bull, the celebrated scholar of International Relations, has also commented that "Ali Mazrui is not only the most distinguished writer to have emerged from independent Black Africa and the most penetrating and discriminating expositor of the ideology of the Third World, but he is also a most illuminating interpreter of the drift of world politics."[31] Even in Bull's formulation there is nothing to suggest that Mazrui is merely an expert of Third World or African issues, although he emerges from the area described as such. Mazrui is indeed a scholar who has, to use the words of one leading African diplomat, "succeeded in broadening his perspective without adulterating his African perspective."[32] In its scope, Mazruiana is therefore global. Its flagship concept, *the triple heritage*, captures this very fact.[33]

But even if the primary focus of Mazruiana were the Third World, would that become a good enough reason for ignoring its relevance to IR given that the largest majority of people inhabiting this planet are not in the first or second, but in the Third World? This is probably a more profound question for which a genuine answer has to be sought from a non-Western perspective.[34] While the scope of Mazruiana is global, its perspective could rightly be regarded as bottom-up. Even so, again, if Mazruiana's primary focus on the Third World cannot warrant its obscurity in IR, neither should its perspective lead to such a conclusion.

Still others may claim that Mazruiana is too focused on domestic politics. This is also a less defensible claim for the same reason indicated above — Mazruiana seems to have an inherent aversion to narrow specialization. But if we assume for a moment that even this claim were true, let us ask again, would it be sufficient to justify the marginalization of Mazruiana? Our answer is certainly not. A cursory review of the history of international relations thought clearly indicates that the discipline of IR emerged as a result of a cumulative synthesis of the works of political philosophers most of which had almost nothing to do with international relations, or inter-state relations, in the modern sense of the term. In fact, in some cases what these philosophers had written about the nature of relationship among individuals in domestic politics (of a hypothetical society) was later extrapolated to relations among contemporary states. The assumption of anarchy, which forms the bedrock of contemporary IR theories, is the most outstanding case in point.

A critic may also argue in the reverse stating to the effect that Mazruiana is a vast body of knowledge encompassing not only international relations and comparative politics but stretching as far away as sociology, socio-linguistics and literary studies. The short response to this statement could take on the form of: so what? To define Mazruiana in such broad terms is not far from the truth, but to imply that therefore it does not have plenty to offer to IR makes much less sense.

Unfortunately it is true that it has become almost conventional in the academia to consider as great a body of work that is narrowly focused "while discussion of the big picture is relegated to cocktail party conversation."[35] But I argue here that whereas narrow specialization is not undesirable, it had not always been the most intellectually enlightening. This is even truer in the age of globalization. In this respect, one observer seems to be right on the mark when he suggested: "We have to learn not only to have specialists but also people whose specialty is to spot the strong interactions and the entanglements of the different dimensions..."[36] Jon Huer had similarly argued in his, *The Fallacies of Social Science: A Critique of the Natural Sci-*

ence Model of Social Analysis:

> There is no way a social scientist can 'know' only 'parts' of his society without knowing the 'whole' of society, although one social scientist knows *more* or *less* about the whole society than another. For a social scientist, unlike a natural scientist, knowing 'parts' of his subject is tantamount to knowing *nothing* about it, for knowledge about parts of society is invalid as knowledge and impossible as knowledge production. It is the whole or nothing in social sciences.[37]

It is therefore fair to conclude that the challenges Mazruiana poses to the established ways of thinking might be the single most important factor that contributed to its "irrelevance".

Mazruiana and Its Critics: Part II

The above discussion reflects some of the general features of Mazruiana, both imagined and real, which are relevant to the appreciation of its relative obscurity in IR. Now I turn to the more specific critiques of Mazruiana. The late Omari Kokole summarized the two predominant views about Mazruiana as follows: "…most readers either intensely like or dislike Mazrui's scholarship."[38] For my present purpose I shall focus exclusively on the rationale of those who intensely dislike Mazruiana. In the course of doing so, I shall nevertheless try not to succumb too easily to the temptations of passing a definitive judgment.

Perhaps Charles Armour's characterization of the purported reason of those who intensely dislike Mazruiana could provide a useful framework for our discussion. The criticism stated below is certainly not a representative of the reaction of the majority of those who are closely familiar with Mazruiana. The ensuing discussion should also be understood in the context of the widespread view that, in the words of Chief Emeka Anyaoku, the former Secretary General of the Common-

Paradigm Lost, Paradigm Regained

wealth: "...the truth is that most authentic deep thinking Africans and non-Africans genuinely interested in understanding the reality...have always valued [Ali Mazrui's] contributions even when they do not share their views."[39] The starkness of Armour's criticism could nevertheless serve as a critical test of Mazruiana. It is in this context that I wish to see if the criticism could be cleared away.

Armour wrote, in a review of one recent book on Mazruiana, that "...Ali Mazrui performs magnificently on the surface but all too often there is a lack of depth, a failure to pause for deeper analysis and persistent use of blanket terminology that he never defines..."[40] If we break down Armour's charges, they boil down to: 1) lack of depth, 2) failure to pause for deeper analysis, and 3) persistent use of blanket terminology that Mazrui never defines. Let us see each of these "failings" one at a time.

First, lack of depth. What is a depth of a scholarship? How deep does an intellectually respectable scholarship need to penetrate into the subject matter? And, most importantly, how is the depth of a scholarship measured? We have not read all of the reviews of Mazrui's multi-faceted works, but if Armour's claim is indeed true even in part, the unavoidable question which arises is: what exactly did these critics mean when they say Mazruiana lacks depth? It may well be that the critics have not provided clear answers to these questions in which case the case automatically closes itself.

A careful examination of Mazruiana reveals that Mazrui is fond of argument by historical analogies and paradoxes, as I shall further discuss later in the book. He is also adept at perceptively making the unfamiliar phenomenon look like familiar. And almost in all of his reasoning Mazrui carefully follows logic. And yet Mazruiana rarely makes use of statistical manipulation, although it does, almost always, support its propositions with fairly indisputable facts and reasoning. Viewed in this light, therefore, what appears to some critics as "lack of depth" might in fact be the critics' insufficient grasp of the intrinsic feature of Mazruiana's methodological orientation and styles of analysis.

To the extent Mazruiana advances clear hypotheses in a verifiable way, the fact that it did not rigorously utilize statistical analysis does not make it lack in depth. As one reviewer of Mazrui's *The Political Sociology of the English Language* put it: "Statistical analyses of language distribution and patterns of usage [are] not found in this book... [But] there are many who might collect and interpret such trends for us, but few can offer so deep and personal a documentation...."[41] The same could be said about Mazrui's other works. And it is in part Mazrui's consistent use of this approach that makes his works both readable and enlightening at the same time.

As indicated in the introductory chapter, Mazrui's style of argument and line of reasoning are closer to deductivism. What this also means is that to the extent quantitative analysis is generally unsuitable for deductivism, Mazruiana is consistently scientific in a methodological sense; a failure to use quantitative and statistical analysis does not in itself mean that an intellectual output produced under the circumstances is unscientific. What Bertrand Russell observed a long time ago is as valid today as it was then, and it is relevant to the context of our discussion. He said:

> The part played by measurement and quantity in science is very great, but is, I think, sometimes overestimated. Mathematical technique is powerful, and men of science are naturally anxious to be able to apply it whenever possible; but a law may be quite scientific without being quantitative.[42]

Therefore it is fair to say that much of the criticism leveled at Mazruiana in this regard is most probably attributable to the inattention to this stylistic and methodological fact. Response to the second charge, i.e. failure to pause for deeper analysis becomes necessary only if the first charge, that is lack of depth, is proved to be true. As I indicated above in relation to the first question, Mazruiana is not shallow and that the critics' misreading of it might have itself arisen out conflating a methodological issue with one pertaining to style of analysis.

It should also be pointed out here that given the vastness of Mazrui's intellectual outputs what irritates critics may in fact be only "his failure to pause". In his colorful scholarly career, Mazrui has over 500 publications.[43] But it must be stressed that there is not any incontrovertible proof which indicates that there needs to be necessarily an inverse relationship between the quality of scholarly works and the pace at which they are produced.[44]

The third charge of persistent use of undefined blanket terminology is the most serious one. Compared to the preceding two, however, it is also a charge that is easier to refute. One of the attractions of Mazruiana is its clarity. Bewildering abstraction is alien to it. Not only is Mazrui fond of simplification without simplicity, he is a genius in converting the most abstract philosophical concept, be it from Edmund Burke, David Hume, Thomas Hobbes, or Jean Jacques Rousseau, John Stuart Mill or John Locke, into a comprehensible and operational language.

In fact, it can be said that along with originality, clarity of expression is an outstanding greatest gift of Mazrui that sets him apart from most of his contemporaries. This point is further substantiated in chapter four. One can therefore simply dispose of the charge that Mazruiana uses a blanket terminology. Mazruiana is not perfect; it must have, like any other body of social knowledge, limitations of its own. However, even insistence on its limitations must be viewed as suggestive merely of the limits within which it can be admired.

Conclusion

The relative neglect of Mazruiana in IR, despite the former's "cornucopia of ideas"[45] is not due to its lack of depth. One explanation perhaps pertains to the fact that Mazruiana, despite its unquestionable profundity, is not sufficiently socialized into the abstraction and obfuscation so common in the social sciences. The accessibility of Mazrui's writings is a widely remarked upon subject. It seems that the following statement by Salim A. Salim, Secretary General of the OAU, reflects the views of most of those familiar with Mazruiana: "[Mazrui's] analytical capacity to traverse historical time, to capture the subtleties of multicultural dynamics, and at the same time to remain concrete and comprehensible is, indeed, outstanding."[46] Recently Kofi Annan, the Secretary General of the UN, similarly lavished a deserved praise on Ali Mazrui as "a visionary African scholar and intellectual whose writings I have long admired."[47]

A more plausible, if also only partial, explanation for Mazruina's relative obscurity is the privileged status of certain issues, regions and approaches in the academic field, what Kevin Dunn has recently called "Western provincialism in IR"[48]. Mazrui's own recent observation about his place in the discipline is an accurate reflection of this sorry fact. Without bitterness or rancor, but rather with a little sense of humor, he noted the following in one of his annual personal newsletters:

> The International Studies Association held its 1999 convention in Washington, D. C. Specialists on International Development had launched a special award for a Distinguished Senior Scholar in the field. I was honored to receive the 1999 Distinguished Award. At the session there were moving tributes from colleagues…It was more than I deserved. However, the organizers had over-estimated the size of my fan-club in the International Studies Association!! So the hall was much larger than the crowd that turned up.!![49]

A prominent IR scholar, Craig Murphy, has recently remarked that although "[m]ore than one out of ten people [in the world] are

Paradigm Lost, Paradigm Regained

African and [m]ore than one out of ten nations are African, I would warrant that fewer than one in a hundred university lecturers on International Relations (IR) given in Europe or North America even mention the continent."[50] Murphy added, "a certain kind of contemporary realist tells us that this is because IR is about the politics of powerful states."[51] Indeed, a leading figure of the neorealist school in IR had an occasion to assert exactly that: "a theory of international politics is a theory of great power behavior."[52] But given, for instance, possession of weapons of mass destruction even by states that could not be regarded as great powers in any accepted sense of the word, the formulation of theory of international politics in these terms appears quite unpersuasive or, at least, is outdated. In this respect, the same logic, which Mazrui had outlined in 1977 for economic relations among states, is applicable to the equation in the military sphere.[53]

But the fact remains that Africa has been estranged from IR theories and this is not surprising at all since, as Kevin Dunn put it, "[t]he West's authorship of IR theory is a hegemonic practice which closes out other possible readings/writings of world politics."[54]

It must be realized, however, that a theory of international politics would make more practical sense if it starts from the premise that the era in which a great military power would also be *ipso facto* economic power or vice versa had faded into oblivion. As Georg Sorensen persuasively argued, in the post-Cold War world, exclusive focus [in IR] on the great powers is no longer sufficient.[55] Most analysts agree, for instance, that it is perilous to disregard North Korea's nuclear programs or its external behavior in this context simply because the country is not 'a great power'.

Yet that the Third World had over the decades become a focus of more scholarly studies, especially after parts of it began to throw some geo-political weight on the superpowers, is a fact. When the times changed in this way, the intellectuals had also to reflect this "with at the very least discarding the social prejudice that only the West was worth studying, since only the West had historically progressed."[56]

Still some political scientists assume that even if the "uncivilized" nations are now subject to study, they require a different set of theory. For example, the authors of the theory of complex interdependence once suggested "a dualistic approach" where the utility of realism was great for the study of "conflictual politics among not too civilized states", while an alternative model of "complex interdependence" was deemed more relevant to the politics among the developed, democratic states.[57] Others have similarly talked about what they called "a liberal core and a realist periphery".[58]

The theory of complex interdependence may well be irrelevant or, to put it more accurately, inadequate for understanding international relations of many of the countries in the Southern hemisphere. Yet developments in the post Cold-War period have sufficiently demonstrated that the South has no monopoly of "conflictual politics". Neither can one sustain the implicit claim that that "primitive interdependence" or "feudo-imperial interdependence" have no bearing on issues of peace and war in the context of the inter-state relations of the states in the South.[59]

In so far as what lay behind the brutalities in Bosnia and Kosovo or Somalia and Rwanda was tribalism in one form or another, the conflicts in themselves are not essentially different. As Mazrui put it more recently, albeit in a different context, "[a]gainst the background of the primordial outbreaks of conflict in the former Yugoslavia, it is clear that 'tribalism' can easily wear a white face as a black one."[60] We could feel almost certain, however, that the authors of the "theory of complex interdependence" did not have Bosnias or Kosovos in mind when they advocated the utility of realism for the study of "conflictual politics among not too civilized states."

Behind the neorealist's hegemonic conceptual model and the complex interdependence theorists' binarist discourse seems to be, in the final analysis, an implicit suggestion that the study of "world politics" is, or should be, the sole task of those scholars whose views uncritically reflect the predominant ideas and /or those who are affiliated with the ideology of the developed states or great powers and that perspectives other than these should be, if possible, domesticated or otherwise they should be neutralized or be ignored as irrelevant. If this is indeed so, then, we must be closer to discovering an important dimension of the explanation for the systematic marginalization of works which, although global in their scope, represent a bottom-up view of the world, such as one that looks at the world from an African perspective,[61] and which, in so doing, threaten to shake the very foundation of the prevailing "regime of truth."

In closing, I wish to reiterate that there is no justification whatsoever for the major theories of IR to neglect Africa. But, it should be admitted, Africa's marginality perpetuates itself as much as a result of the monopoly of the field by "great power IR" theorists as it is a result of the failure of "the Other" to challenge this monopoly, however entrenched the monopoly is, not only by bringing to focus the relevance of "Other" issues to contemporary IR theories,[62] but also—and even more importantly—by actively engaging in the process of discursive formations. Mazruiana is a landmark contribution in both areas.

1 Mazrui (1964).
2 For a comprehensive list see Bemath (1998).
3 Back in 1975, a comparative Africanist was how Mazrui described himself. See Mazrui (1977a: 236).
4 Harbeson (1998: 25).
5 See Mazrui (1989b: 170).
6 Mazrui (1977a: 69-81).
7 Harbeson (1998: 27).
8 Bull (1966: 361)
9 Alamin Mazrui (1998: 155-172).
10 Mazrui (1998e: 10).
11 See Mazrui (1982b: 250-253).
12 Mazrui (1981a: 18).
13 Mazrui (1998e: 9-10).
14 Mazrui (1975a: 1-37).

15 See Mazrui (1989b: 155-171).
16 See Mazrui (1986a: 14); Mazrui (1995e: 338).
17 See Feldman (2001: 343-371). See Mazrui (1986: 4); Mazrui (1995d: 338).
18 Mazrui (1975a: 465).
19 Ufumaka (1994: 55).
20 Sawere (1998: 269-289).
21 Mowoe (2001: 145-155).
22 Salem (2001: 63-101).
23 Ufumaka (1994: 55).
24 Waever (1997: 4).
25 Mazrui (1990c: 145-178).
26 Sawere (1998: 274).
27 Mazrui (1974a: 59).
28 Mazrui (1974a: 80).
29 Mazrui (1985a: 186).
30 Leys (1968).
31 Bull (1978).
32 Anyaoku (2000: 23).
33 For elaboration of the concept see Mazrui (1986a). See also chapter seven of this book.
34 For such an attempt from a European perspective see Waever (1998: 687-727).
35 Friedman (2000: 28).
36 Friedman (2000: 28).
37 Huer (1990: 108).
38 Kokole (1998b: 15).
39 Anyaoku, 'Bridging the Gap', Q-News, July 2000, p. 23.
40 Armour (2001: 717).
41 American Anthropologist (1976).
42 Russell (2001: 47).
43 See Bemath (1998).
44 Kokole (1998: 8).
45 Legum (1967).
46 'Mazrui: The Tributes' *Q-News*, July 2000, p. 24.
47 'Mazrui: The tributes', *Q-News* , July 2000, p. 24.
48 Dunn (2001: 15).
49 Mazrui (2000d: 10).
50 Murphy (2001:ix).
51 Murphy (2001:ix).
52 Quoted in Holsti (1998: 27).
53 Mazrui (1977d: 3).
54 Dunn (2001: 3).
55 Sorensen (1997: 256).
56 Wallerstein (1991: 844-845).
57 Mentioned in Waever (1997: 30).

58 See Goldgeier and McFaul (1992: 491).
59 The terms in the inverted commas are from Mazrui (1980a: 64). For elaboration, see chapter 6 of this book.
60 Mazrui (2001a: 98).
61 Mazrui (1992a: 1).
62 Examples of this type of work include Dunn and Shaw (2001); Kalu (2001).

3. Mazruiana and the New IR

Introduction

In chapter two I suggested that Mazruiana is a body of knowledge with unquestionable relevance to International Relations (IR). In this chapter I focus in more specific terms on one phase in the development of IR, the new IR. Here I begin by defining the new IR. I describe the features it shares with Mazruiana and their expressions after that.

The new IR can be defined first in terms of what it is not. The new IR is the opposite of the old IR. The old IR centered for the most part on the debate between the proponents of political realism and liberalism, with the predominance of the agenda set by the former. The old IR has been the predominant and largely unchallenged form of discourse since the discipline emerged as an independent field of study. From the 1980s, however, social constructivism began to vie for a place alongside the two master narratives. Although it has not yet gained a wider acceptance as an alternative paradigm, social constructivism has presented itself as a formidable challenge to political realism and liberalism, both in their old and present-day variants. It is this enlarged and enriched method of inquiry and research program, which I have labeled the New IR. The marker "new" in the new IR thus signifies both the addition of a *new* paradigm to IR and the re*newal* of the old as the result. I shall discuss below the relationship between Mazruiana and the new paradigm.

The Social Constructivism of Mazruiana

Although social constructivism began to appear in IR literature as a solid and potentially alternative perspective on world affairs only in the 1980s, many philosophers had generations ago articulated, albeit less systematically, a line of thought which would be accepted today as constructivist. Some analysts have in fact traced this line of thought to very early times, calling Thucydides the founding father of social constructivism.[1]

Friedrich Nietzsche, the 19th century German philosopher, condemned many of the philosophers who preceded him, but most notably Socrates, for being "social constructivists," denouncing them for "their lack of historical sense, their hatred of the very idea of becoming, their Egypticism."[2] He elaborated what he meant thus: "We decided to accept the evidence of the senses—when we were still learning to sharpen them, arm them, think them through to the end. The rest is abortion and not-yet-science."[3] There are also scholars who trace the social constructivist thought in IR, especially in its present form, to a more recent period.[4]

In any case a variety of social constructivisms have been identified. John Ruggie, for instance, classified them into neoclassical, postmodernist and naturalistic.[5] Among these, postmodernist social constructivism approximates my usage of the term in this book. Ruggie points out that in the postmodernist social constructivism:

> [t]he linguistic construction of subjects is stressed, as a result of which discursive practices constitute the ontological primitives, or the foundational units of reality and analysis. Little hope is held out for a

legitimate social science. In its place, a 'hegemonic discourse' is seen to impose a 'regime of truth,' instituted through disciplinary powers in both senses of that term.[6]

Postmodernist social constructivism maintains that there are things that are "real" only because we think, or we are made to think, that they are so. It thus postulates that "reality" can be and often is constructed. Yet, even though "reality" is constructed, the consequences of our actions with regard to that "reality" would not nevertheless be unreal, for, in other words, "they become a part of the objective world by virtue of their existence in the intersubjectivity of relevant groups or people."[7]

It also follows that in the social world there is no absolute truth, but only "received truth" and that there is no external, objective reality, but only our own subjective interpretation or understanding. The emphasis on the instrumentality of ideas for social change as well as the fluidity of identity and interest is therefore the principal feature of social constructivism.

In the above senses, a constructivist should denote a person who primarily deconstructs "reality" rather than one who constructs it; a constructivist debunks ideas that are believed not to fit empirical reality, ideas that are too abstract and thus erase reality and/or ideas that are extrapolations of European prejudices.[8] And yet dialectics inseparably link both the processes of construction and deconstruction. Deconstruction is itself a form of a constructive act. What Brenda Marshall said about postmodernism in general also applies to social constructivism:

> Postmodernism is about history. But not the kind of 'History' that lets us think we can know the past. History in the postmodern moment becomes histories and questions. It asks: Whose history gets told? In whose name? For what purpose? Postmodernism is about histories not told, retold, untold. History as it never was. Histories forgotten, hidden, invisible, considered unimportant, changed, eradicated. It is

about the refusal to see history as linear, as leading straight up to today in some recognizable manner.[9]

Mazruiana has for the most part preoccupied itself with representing histories in the above sense, thereby revealing the fact that "reality" has indeed a pluralistic and plastic nature. In this, Mazruiana views ontological primacy or the data we receive through our senses with an air of skepticism. Much in the same way, Pauline Rosenau has, as quoted by Tony Porter, characterized postmodernism as involving:

> A rejection of method based on reason, of the notion that the mind apprehends an already existing reality, and of the hermeneutic goal of discovering preexisting meaning...
> 'deconstruction involves demystifying a text, tearing it apart to reveal its internal, arbitrary hierarchies, and its presuppositions.'[10]

One of the works in which Mazrui clearly outlines the contours of his brand of social constructivism is *Cultural Amnesia, Cultural Nostalgia and False Memory*. He elaborated the theme in relation to social memory and identity formation:

> Four processes of social memory are involved in identity formation. These basic processes are, quite simply, preservation, selection, elimination, and invention. What is remembered is, in our sense, preserved in the memory. But it is inevitable that a *selection* process takes place—for the social memory will not remember every detail. Positive selection may lead to *nostalgia*, a desire, if not to re-enact, to recapture the happier past in spirit. Negative selection by the memory, on the other hand, may lead to social or cultural *amnesia*—a forgetting of a past deemed to be unhappy or in some sense inglorious. The fourth process is the invention of the past—believing in a past which never was. Logically, there is a question as to whether this is a *memory* at all or whether it is something else.[11]

Mazruiana appropriates and re-writes African history and contests much of the Eurocentric ideas in it. In the same way, it almost always starts with a received truth, an assertion based on a particular community's viewpoint, and then debunks that "received truth," challenging its extrapolation onto another part.

Starting from the premise that all claims to truth are questionable, social constructivism stresses that knowledge is not atemporal. On language, it emphasizes its constitutive role; language is not merely a tool through which we tell stories, it is, most importantly, a means of creating meaning and identity and communicating it in symbols, and, in this sense, is related to power. A concern with such issues is a recurrent theme in Mazruiana. A good example is the case of the Algerian liberation war where Mazrui successfully deconstructs the Eurocentricity of the way the story was told.[12]

After persuasively relating how the Algerians changed history, Mazrui recounted how a similar, if more concrete, role was played by Afghan Mujahidin in changing world history.[13]

Also significant in Mazruiana's constructivism is, as suggested above, the pervasive interest in language both as the subject of analysis and as, in his own words, a "tool for a verbal combat."[14] Consistent with the inquiries that are structured within the constructivist framework, Mazruiana similarly breaks disciplinary boundaries, as elaborated in the previous chapter. To illuminate some of the features of Mazruiana's social constructivism and how it is expressed, I shall now turn to the consideration of a few more examples from Mazruiana texts.

In one of his earlier works, published in *American Political Science Review* in 1963, Mazrui called attention to the emerging trend in American scholarship which took the form of "projecting their own estimate of important American thinkers onto the rest of the world."[15]

Mazrui aspired to deconstruct a received truth also in his essay, *Ancient Greece in African Thought,* a publication based on his inaugural lecture when he was first appointed full professor at Makerere

University in Uganda in 1967. In it he launched a counter-offensive in response to the issue surrounding the Africanness of Egypt's civilization suggesting, "in a sense, it is easier to prove that ancient Egypt was African than to prove that ancient Greece was European."[16]

Mazrui follows the same method of analysis in *The Africans: A Triple Heritage*.[17] In one instance, he asked: what is Africa? On this question, he maintained, adopting what could easily be regarded as the perspective of critical geopolitics, that although the scholarship had paid greater attention to "the artificiality of the borders of African states, the border of the continent itself was not much less artificial."[18] He contested the notion that Yemen, which is separated from the African landmass by a "stone's throw," was regarded not part of Africa while Madagascar or Mauritius with their respective distance of 500 and 1000 miles from Africa's coastline qualified as part of Africa.[19]

In another book whose constructivist premise is evident from its very title, *Cultural Engineering and Nation Building in East Africa*[20], Mazrui underscored the relevance of the issue of hegemony of discourse for a fuller understanding of political "reality." In this book, he critically interrogated why "the oral tradition of living inhabitants was not a far better indication of the reality of Africa's past than the vivid and romantic accounts of European explorers."[21] Synthesizing his earlier arguments on the subject, Mazrui concluded recently: "European imperialism in Africa played havoc with the African memory—initiating new forms of amnesia, nostalgia, and false memories."[22]

Mazruiana's focus is not, however, geared merely towards "the truth" received from "the other." It also calls attention to the role of ideas in the context of post-independence Africa. It maintains that the "representation" of "reality" almost always corresponds to the "prevailing regime of truth," whether that truth is produced internally or externally.[23] In addition to his works that specifically deal with Africa, Mazrui has been formulating ideas which have broader and direct relevance to contemporary IR. In them, too, his constructivist inclinations are unmistakably clear. Some of these ideas are discussed below.

Mazruiana on the Nature of the International System

On one occasion, Mazrui advanced (and substantiated) a hypothesis on the stability of non-egalitarian systems, asking why "systems of gross social inequalities have often lasted much longer without tension than systems of relative egalitarianism." His conclusion was that "a good deal may depend upon the degree of consensus behind the inequalities rather than the degree of inequality itself."[24]

Such hypotheses are not without significance for making sense of the relative stability of a hierarchical international system. The same insight could be made to apply to the analysis of the turmoil that engulfed many states in the wake of the end of the Cold War. Intrastate conflicts of this nature have indeed recently attracted the attention of IR analysts, whereas the subject has in the past been mainly the preserve of the disciplines of comparative politics and area studies. Undoubtedly, Mazruiana's thesis about the relationship between consensus and political stability is quite relevant to further our understanding of the revival of tribalism in different parts of the globe. From Rwanda to Yugoslavia and the former Soviet Union, it seems that it is such questioning of the "long accepted legitimacy of the criteria of stratification" which brought about confrontations between different groups in these states leading to the eventual collapse of some of them. As the tragic events in Somalia also reaffirmed, it is perhaps not cultural diversity *per se* that is the cause of violent tribalism. Neither is it solely attributable to the scarcity of resources, as some have claimed.[25]

One of the remarkable features of Mazruiana is that it had anticipated many of the issues that were later to preoccupy the works of some IR scholars. Mazruiana's perspective on the religious root of the structure of contemporary world politics articulated in 1975 falls into this category. More than quarter a century later, some IR students echo essentially the same idea with different tone and emphasis.[26]

In his *Social Theory of International Politics* (published in 1999), Alexander Wendt coined the useful concept of ontological security, and defined it as "the human predisposition for a relatively stable expectation about the world around them."[27] Wendt, who is one of the most well-known social constructivists in IR today, went on to clarify the concept as follows: "…along with the need for physical security, this [predisposition] pushes human beings in a conservative homeostatic direction, and to seek out recognition of their standing from their society."[28] Mazrui has one novel published under his name titled, *The Trial of Christopher Okigbo*.[29] In this novel, published almost 40 years earlier than Alexander Wendt's book, Mazrui addresses the issue of "ontological security" in the form of a self-reflection by one of his fictional characters, a man named Hamisi Salim, who is killed by a car accident in Kenya and is pondering why in the hypothetical world of life after death, things bear such resemblance with the ones in the world of the life before death. Mazrui gives his account of Hamisi's self-reflection in these terms: "I suppose the answer lies in the simple proposition that half the total sum of human happiness consists in the sense of security afforded by the familiar."[30]

In the same book, Mazrui introduces through the mouths of his fictional characters a theme which is akin to a synthesis of the major propositions of what IR scholars call game theory, which represents, in the words of Von Neumann, the author of the theory, a situation of a "conflict of interests resolved by the accumulative choices players make while trying to anticipate each other."[31] Mazrui's theme in this instance seems also to run in a parallel course with the debate that has continued between, on the one hand, those IR scholars who argue that international actors, primarily states, are more interested in relative gains than in absolute gains in their interactions with one another and, on the other hand, those who believe otherwise. In Mazrui's formulation a game is played between two teams in an attempt to establish "a monotheistic lead," and once one side achieves the lead, it shifts to "the strategy of defense" so as to preserve the lead which is "aesthetically more satisfying."[32] On one level, the story of the contest between the two teams seems to parallel a rivalry either of the deadly type such as that which existed between the superpowers during the Cold War period, or that which is less so. The contestants are not interested in absolute gains—that is, the maximization of gains as much as possible. They are content with achieving preponderance, however small the margin.

In his later works, Mazrui underscored again, in the context of what he called social mobility, the significance of relative gains as opposed to absolute gains. Defining social mobility as meaning "not only more ability to improve the lot of the poorer sections of a particular society, but also the possibility of narrowing the gap of affluence between the poorest and the richest," Mazrui argued, for a social mobility to take place, "the poor must not only be earning a little more than what they used to; they must also have reduced the gap in income between themselves and those who are wealthier. If the gap is maintained, the sense of deprivation continues."[33]

Some IR scholars have similarly argued that states seek relative gain, or "a margin of superiority", rather than pursuing absolute gain. However, in the case of inter-state relations, obviously, it is not the "aesthetic satisfaction" which fuels the drive for a relative gain over the rival. Instead, it is the "security dilemma" which motivates them to maximize their relative power. Such a notion also reinforces another Mazruiana hypothesis—relation of absolute inequality is much more stable than one that is of parity—whether the game is in play or not. And the game in a situation like this could thus be regarded as, to use the parlance of the game theoretic model, a zero-sum game.

Globalization

Globalization, or the villagization of the world as Mazrui referred to it in 1974,[34] is a related theme that has been adequately addressed in Mazruiana. Before the talk about globalization was in vogue, Mazrui was writing about it in terms that seem to have a perfect resemblance to the lexicon of the most well-known authorities on the subject today. Back in 1974, Mazrui observed that the increase in individual awareness and the revolution in technology have combined their forces "to introduce the beginnings of shared values, shared tastes, and shared images among the peoples of this planet."[35]

James Rosenau, the veteran scholar of international relations, coined in 1995 the concept of "skill revolution."[36] To him, with the end of the Cold War, the skills of individuals have significantly increased. In his own words, "[p]eople have become increasingly more competent in assessing where they fit in international affairs and how their behavior can be aggregated into significant collective outcomes."[37] Mazruiana's position on this score would seem that there is such a skill revolution is beyond any shadow of doubt. And yet this revolutionary process did not start with the end of the Cold War. The recent revolution in communications technology has surely deepened the changes, making them more pronounced. But the post-Cold War developments in this regard represent a quantitative leap, not a qualitative one. The perspective thus adopted by Mazrui takes the process of skill revolution at least as far back as the Second World War. Mazrui explained this theme in some detail in relation to Africa in his, *The 'Other' as Self Under a Cultural Dependency*.[38]

The idea of convergence gained wider currency with the collapse of communism, as most notably articulated in Francis Fukuyama's "the end of history" thesis. But it is evident that the end of the Cold War did not really bring about a genuine political convergence. In this regard,

Larry Diamond has argued not long ago that it is useful to differentiate between what he labeled "electoral democracy" and "liberal democracy." According to him, the two visibly divergent trends following the collapse of Communism in the former Soviet Union and Eastern Europe are the spread of electoral rights and the continued disrespect for liberties that are supposed to be a postulation for a meaningful exercise of them.[39] In spite of the proliferation of this form of "illiberal democracy," and perhaps even because of it, Mazrui's idea of cultural convergence throws a useful light on the phenomenon. This theme is treated later in the chapter.

To return to the discussion of globalization, Mazrui defined the phenomenon on one occasion as "consisting of processes which lead towards global interdependence and increasing rapidity of exchange across vast distance."[40] Elsewhere he further elaborated the definition: "[G]lobalization consists of those trends in the world which are fostering, wittingly or unwittingly, such tendencies as economic interdependence on a global scale, cross-cultural awareness, and global institution building to regulate both inter human relations and the exploitation of the world resources."[41] But unlike the many other experts of globalization who saw the process of convergence as genuinely emerging, or at any rate accelerating in the past two decades, Mazrui saw it as a longstanding phenomenon that emerged much earlier. Mazrui recounted the different stages of this process in *From Slave Ship to Space Ship*.[42] In his, *Pretender to Universalism: Western Culture in the Globalizing Age*, Mazrui further elucidated how the process of globalization was fueled by the forces of religion, technology, economy, and empire.[43] The paradoxes of globalization, most particularly in its present stage, also did not escape the attention of Mazrui. This he summarized in what he called the two faces of hegemonic globalization, namely homogenization (making all of us look familiar) and hegemonization (making one of us the boss).[44] As for what he called the forms of globalization, his classifications are: comprehensive, economic, and informational.[45]

The Clash of Civilizations

Mazrui has directly addressed the clash of civilizations as conceptualized and articulated by Samuel Huntington.[46] Mazrui had also advanced more than twenty-five years ago an idea which can easily relate to Huntington's thesis. I shall begin here with the older version of Mazruiana's formulation of the clash of civilizations in relation to what he called "the theory of convergence." Huntington's idea of the clash of civilizations has been so often discussed that a detailed exposition of it is hardly necessary. As shortly as I can summarize it, the major elements of the thesis are these: 1) there are fundamental differences between civilizations (which are classified into seven or eight); 2) as a result of globalization there would be more interaction between them and this would lead to increased civilizational consciousness; and; 3) therefore, they would clash.

In his "theory of cultural convergence," Mazrui discussed the issues relating to conflicts among cultural, national, or ideological groups. The process of convergence passes through the stages of coexistence, contact, compromise, and coalescence. In the course of the transition from one stage to another, conflict plays a crucial part. For, "it is the cumulative experience of conflict resolution that deepens the degree of integration in a given society."[47] Such cumulative experience in conflict resolution could also lay the basis for "integration" in the future by supplying the power of precedent and enhanced awareness of reciprocal dependence.[48]

Although Mazrui's focus in the above analysis was centered on nation building, the conclusion which can be drawn from it has wider relevance and implications for international relations and the idea of the clash of civilizations. Let us look at each of them one at a time.

The notion of reciprocal-dependence, which is one of the building blocks of Mazruiana's "theory of cultural convergence," rhymes with the sub-school of International Relations known as "interdependence liberalism." This school maintains that "a high division of labor in the international economy increases interdependence between states, and this discourages and reduces violent conflict between states."[49] Similarly, Mazruiana's idea appears to have some affinity with "institutional liberalism," for which "[i]nternational institutions help promote cooperation between states and thereby help alleviate the lack of trust between states and states' fear of each other, which are considered to be the traditional problems associated with international anarchy."[50]

Some would say that a society without conflict is like a society of ants. Mazrui also seems in the above excerpt to suggest that in its consequences conflict is not always undesirable, although perhaps not to the extent implied by the preceding metaphor. In any case Mazrui asked at what stage in the process of transition violence becomes more pronounced. His answer was:

> Whereas in relations within a single country it is the stage between contact and compromise that has a high potentiality for conflict among compatriot ethnic groups, in relations among nation-states it is very often the stage between compromise and coalescence. In other words, the subprocess of convergence is precisely the stage that carries both the greatest promise and the highest tensions.[51]

What emerges from a closer examination of the above passage is that Mazruiana's view is incompatible with Huntington's idea of "the clash of civilizations." In view of the perquisites of such a "clash" as well as its mechanism and dynamics, one important conclusion can be drawn from the foregoing discussion. But first let us spell out the premises on which it is based.

A clash between different entities by definition presupposes contact between them. There cannot be interdependence between these entities if they have no contacts in the first place. But two or more entities could have a minimal contact without any measure of shared interdependence. It must be added, however, that it is not merely the level of interdependence but the nature of interdependence as well which define issues of conflict and cooperation between collective entities. The convergence or divergence between the values of the entities is also not without relevance. The inescapable conclusion is, therefore, that it is the initial contact that generates conflict. Framed in this way, a clash of civilizations could be viewed as something that first happened quite long ago for the simple reason that major civilizations of the world came into contact with one another initially not in the 1990s. Nor was it after the end of the Cold War. The initial contact took place much earlier. In fact, it can be argued that the origin of the contact and eventual clash between distinct civilizations could be traced back to the year 264 B. C. when the great struggle between Rome and Carthage began.[52] The history of human civilizations is the history of contacts, clashes and conflicts between them as well as their resolutions through a variety of means.

One of the works in which Mazruiana first confronted Huntington's clash of civilizations thesis more directly is *The UN and the Muslim World*.[53] In it, Mazrui registered his disagreement with Huntington "about the nature of that clash and about how old it is," and added: "the clash of civilizations did not begin with the end of the Cold war but is much older" and that "the chief cultural transgressor has throughout been the Western world."[54] In his later work, Mazrui further sharpened his criticism of the idea of the clash of civilizations on what he called conceptual, factual, and temporal grounds.[55]

In short, Mazruiana maintains that the cumulative experience of conflict resolutions, which is at the disposal of civilizations, make it less rather than more likely that future conflicts will be fought along civilization lines. The very existence of such "lines" is itself highly dubious. As H. G. Wells observed about eighty years ago: "[p]eople will use such a word as race in the loosest manner, and base the most preposterous generalizations on it. They will speak of a 'British' race or of a 'European' race. But nearly all the European nations are confused mixtures of brownish, dark-white, white, and Mongolian elements."[56]

It should be clear, however, that Huntington's definition of a civilization is not based solely on racial catgories, although race constitutes an important dimension of it. It ought to be remembered in this connection also that civilizational identities could be constructed in the same way as national or ethnic identities, and conflicts among them could become in this way a self-fulfilling prophecy. Therefore, the power to fulfill itself is probably the most profound and potential danger that inheres in the steadily growing popularity of the clash of civilizations thesis. This theme is discussed at length in chapter five.

In addition to the clash civilizations, the idea of international interventions is one of the related themes that have captured the attention of IR scholars in recent years, especially following the events in Somalia, Rwanda, and the former Yugoslavia. Mazrui addressed this issue in his *On Heroes and Uhuru-Worship* in 1967 in the context of the United Nations intervention in the Congo.[57] Mazrui argued that what happened in the Congo in this case was a harbinger of the erosion of national sovereignty since this was a case of "globalizing" a domestic problem out of the conviction that "the stability of the world was rapidly becoming indivisible."[58]

State Collapse

The phenomena of state failures, touched upon earlier, have in recent years caught the attention of IR scholars and practitioners. After observing the widespread intellectual effort to comprehend these phenomena, Mazrui offered a definition of state in terms of its six functions: control over territory, resources, infrastructure, revenue collection, social services as well as governance, and law and order.[59] He then maintained, "we may get longer notice of a State in decay if we worked out indicators of performance in all these areas."[60]

Among the many others, this is one clear illustration of the fact that providing clear definitions of key concepts, even for those that we think we know their meaning is a major characteristic of Mazruiana, as I pointed out also in the previous chapter. Political scientists sometimes overlook the need to define state failure in such operational and verifiable terms. There is often the mistaken assumption that those who read and write literature on state failure understand and share the meaning. Consequently, most definitions, if they are provided at all, tend to be overly abstract or vague.

A more substantive significance of the Mazruiana conceptualization on state failure lies, first, in the fact that its conception is enabling to clarify the quality of statesness in measurable terms. Decades ago, J. P. Nettl suggested that the indiscriminate use of the concept of state be re-evaluated, stating also that the continued use of the term "state" in the context of developing countries represents a form of conceptual underdevelopment within the social sciences.[61] Nettl's suggestion thus seemed to have found a positive response in Mazruiana. Mazrui's definition makes the abstract concept of a state so measurable that we can speak of the degree of statesness with more concreteness and precision.

The second aspect of the usefulness of this approach is that it introduces a new dimension to the well-known Weberian definition of state by approaching the concept from a different angle. Max Weber defined state as a "…corporate group that has compulsory jurisdiction, exercises continuous organization, and claims a monopoly of force over a territory and its population including all action taking place in the area of its jurisdiction."[62] Weber's definition is focused on the "means" of state.

On the other hand, Mazrui defined state comprehensively in terms of the functions it is supposed to perform rather than in terms of the means to this end. At a time when there is a major concern that a wave of state failures may lie ahead, the Mazruiana perspective seems to offer a useful insight into the phenomena. The fact that virtually all states claim the monopoly of the legitimate use of force did not save some of them from "failing." Thus, whereas the Weberian definition does help us identify a state that has or has not completely "failed" or an entity that is no longer a state, it is not of much value for identifying a state that is "failing." But Mazruiana's approach does help to address the issue of a "decaying" state. Needless to say, the latter approach is based on the core premise that state failure is a process, not an event.

In fact, Mazruiana even goes further by providing the necessary conceptual tools for determining how much a state has failed and why. In his *The Frankenstein State and Uneven Sovereignty*, Mazrui introduced yet another important dimension to Weber's definition of state by insisting that for a state to be a state there are other things which it must do in addition to the important perquisite of the assertion of the monopoly of the legitimate use of physical force; it has to also assert "the monopoly of the legitimate use of *intellectual* power, or of avenues of opinion. A desire for concentrated physical force leads on to a desire for orchestrated intellectual power."[63]

On the Concept of Power

Susan Strange is regarded as the founding mother of the field of international political economy in Britain.[64] In her well-known book, *States and Markets* which was published in 1988, she introduced the four structures of power in global political economy—namely, the security structure, the production structure, the financial structure, and the knowledge structure, which she defined respectively as: the framework of power created by the provision of security by some human beings for others; the sum of all the arrangements determining what is produced, by whom and for whom, by what method and on what terms; the sum of all the arrangements governing the availability of credit plus all the factors determining the terms on which currencies are exchanged for one another; what is believed (and the moral conclusions and principles derived from those beliefs); what is known and perceived as understood; and the channels by which beliefs, ideas and knowledge are communicated—including some people and excluding others.[65]

In a manner that seemed to have anticipated Strange's theory, Mazrui laid down these distinctions in his own way even earlier in terms that are less abstract. In other words, in Mazruiana the distinctions are made between these elements of structural power, or in Mazrui's own preferred terminology, the means of communication, along with a lucid substantiation of what a structural power holder could do with it in concrete terms. Mazrui's frame of reference is nevertheless narrower than that of Strange as the former was concerned with North-South relations or, more specifically, the relationship between the United States and the Third World. Mazrui thus explained the growing distance between America and the Third World in terms of the power of the former in the areas of, in his own words: production; the language of the consumer; currency or liquidity; technology; and the English language—the most widely understood tongue in history.[66] In other words, Mazrui's five elements of structural power are: production, consumption, currency or liquidity, technology and (the English) language; correspondingly, for Susan Strange, the four structures of power are that of production, finance, knowledge and security.

Another relevant theme to contemporary discourse on power in world politics relates to "soft power," a concept used by Joseph Nye in 1996.[67] Mazrui dealt with "soft power" in his *World Culture and the Search for Human Consensus*, in relation to what he called a quest for "a purposeful world reform."[68] His argument was based on the premise that "the world needs to be reformed in the direction of three basic values: maximum social justice, more widely distributed economic welfare, and reduced violence, whether actual or imminent."[69] Mazrui then asked the pertinent question of how we could get there. His elaborate answer included "that consensus on a specific set of reforms can best be obtained where people share a framework of social reasoning and social calculation. To convince another person of a new idea requires a common universe of discourse. Persuasion is the art of exploiting mutually familiar predispositions."[70]

Mazruiana's idea of "soft power" is, therefore, broader in its applicability than that of Joseph Nye. Central in Nye's concept of soft power, which he defined as "the ability to achieve desired outcomes in international affairs through attraction rather than coersion",[71] is the power of ideas. For Mazrui, too, ideas occupy an important place in that "their transmission and their internalization are more relevant than the establishment of formal institutions for external control...Thus, even though the transmission of ideas may require some institutions, it is more concerned with *process* than with structure."[72]

In a related way, Mazrui had challenged the predominant view that associated the absence a formal world government with the structure of anarchy. In doing so, he re-emphasized the role of ideas in world politics: "the mechanisms of constraint in the behavior of the big powers, fallible as they are, are an index of the beginnings of political integration in the world. But the integration is at the level of values and their acceptance as the basis of inhibition, rather than at the level of organizational structures."[73] But this form of "integration" could still take place within a context of international stratification or hierarchy.

The End of History

Mazrui's theory of cultural convergence would perhaps become one of the most outstanding contributions he has made to international relations scholarship. This theory is as profound as it is perceptive. For this reason, it may be useful here to return to it for a moment and further elaborate it as a preface to the interpretive analysis of Mazruiana in relation to Francis Fukuyama's famous theory of "the end of history." As indicated earlier in this chapter, Mazrui classified the stages in cultural convergence between two or more social entities into four: coexistence, contact, compromise, and coalescence. The first stage is essentially the "existence" of two or more separate entities whether or not each is aware of the existence of the other. Separate social entities can coexist without any awareness of each other's existence. Then the whole process of convergence begins when contact between them is initiated and interaction gets underway. Once this stage is set, what ensues is "a relationship of compromise that almost invariably entails an intervening period of violent confrontation,"[74] because by this time "the groups or nations still have clearly distinct identities, as well as distinct interests."[75] These sub-processes of compromise and confrontation eventually lead to the fourth stage of coalescence at which stage the process of convergence begins.[76]

While the end of the Cold War provided the context for Francis Fukuyama's idea of "the end of history," Ali Mazrui had earlier written on themes similar to the one surrounding the idea in the recent debates. Mazrui has also more recently clarified his position on Fukuyama's thesis. Here again I start with Mazruiana's earlier formulation. Mazrui suggested about twenty years ago that convergence, be it ideological or cultural, is no guarantee that there will be minimal violence in the world. As he then put it, "...world history reveals not only the tension of cultural differences but also the tragedies of high cultural convergence."[77] He concluded that the explanation for disharmony and brutality, even in the face of homogeneity and cultural convergence, lies in racial privilege.[78] People who are more alike could be more brutal against each other.[79] It was also in a similar context of reasoning that Mazrui coined the concept of *integrated cleavage* in reference to what he said was the disturbing anomaly concerning the tensions of social nearness in horizontal relationships.[80]

Shortly after the end of history became the hot topic of the day in 1993, Mazrui directly addressed the subject questioning both the empirical validity of the thesis and its normative implications. He argued that unless one wanted to throw out the Marxist baby with the Leninist bath water, what has been discredited is only the latter. In addition, Mazrui argued, Marxism is still a potent ideological force as an ethic of distribution and powerful tool as a methodology of analysis. But its credibility as an ideology of development has gone for good, thanks solely to the failure of the experiment with a Leninist version in the former Soviet Union. In another sense too, it is premature to declare the end of Marxism since "it is conceivable that Marxism stands a better chance in Asia, at least in the People's Republic of China, where it has not as yet been abandoned. Democratic centralism is losing its centralism, and we may surely see an increase in the 'democratic' part of democratic centralism."[81]

On the normative side of "the end of history," Mazrui's position was that even if it was true that history has ended in the way described by Fukuyama, there would not be much justification for celebration. He explains this thus: "If history as a quest for the ultimate political order is to come to an end, it can never be satisfied with the message of the West on how to maximize the best in human nature…The 'end of history' has to be a marriage of more than one civilization and more than one standard."[82] As he put it in other words elsewhere: "Cultures should be judged not merely by the heights of achievement to which they have ascended but by the depth of brutality to which they have descended. The measure of culture is not only their virtues but also their vices."[83]

Mazrui further sharpened his perspective in regard to the above in his more recent work, *Pretender to Universalism: Western Culture in the Globalizing Age*, by challenging the end of history from the perspectives of historical relativism, cultural relativism, and comparative empirical performance.[84] His critique of the end of history in his *'Progress': Illegitimate Child of Judeo-Christian Universalism and Western Ethnocentrism* was similarly more focused and refined. Here Mazrui saw a paradox in the end of history thesis. As he explained: "...the choice of the West as the role model or ideal society is ethnocentric, while the idea that all societies are evolving towards the same destination is universalist. The concept of progress is therefore a dialectic between the universalism of a process and the ethnocentrism of destination."[85] In other words, "...Judeo-Christian universalism did indeed illicitly mate with in history—and gave the world a bastard called 'progress.'"[86] I shall return in the fifth chapter to the discussion of "the end of history" from my own personal vantage point.

Conclusion

The forgoing analyses indicate that Mazruiana is relevant to contemporary discourse in IR and that it has a close affinity with the mode of inquiry known as social constructivism. However, Mazruiana's brand of social constructivism has a feature that makes it insusceptible to the one critique usually leveled against the school. Mazruiana is free from bewildering terminologies. In other words, Mazruiana can be regarded as a body of constructivist discourse that is not beset by the seemingly inherent limitation of such discourse.

The constructivist impulse behind Mazruiana is the assumption that the constructed "truth" is not a scientifically justifiable truth (if there is anything as such) but simply a choice made between equally justifiable interpretations. And this constructed "truth" as well as the construction process itself is mediated by social power and rhetoric. This methodological position also resonates well with what E. H. Carr had once said: "the [historical] facts are really not at all like fish on the fishmonger's slab. They are like fish swimming about in a vast and sometimes inaccessible ocean; and what the historian catches will depend, partly on chance, but mainly on what part of the ocean he chooses to fish in and what tackle he chooses to use—these two factors being, of course, determined by the kind of fish he wants to catch."[87]

In the last analysis, the question arises: where could we situate Mazruiana? What is the place of Mazruiana, not only in political science, but in the social sciences in general? These questions call for a substantiation of the related presupposition that Mazruiana is a science. Mazruiana qualifies as a body of scientific knowledge due to the simple, if basic, fact that it is a systematic study of different aspects of human society. It also qualifies as a science since it is an embodiment of a body of testable and verifiable ideas and hypotheses. Let us see more closely, albeit briefly, what each of the above general statements mean.

Positivism demands that for social knowledge to qualify as scientific it should adhere to the method so successfully used in the natural sciences—namely, that it has to be empirical, verifiable, transmissible, general, explanatory, provisional, and non-normative in nature. Mazruiana meets all of these scientific requirements, save the last one. Because Mazruiana is amenable to falsification, it has also no problem in passing the post- positivist test.

Whereas the non-normative nature is often mentioned as one requisite criterion, it is also a prerequisite to which only lip service has often been paid by the vast majority in the social scientific community. Of course some would attribute the social scientists' resistance to normative social science to the view that it is academically an undesirable form of endeavor. Adherence to a non-normative research has nevertheless been one of the persistent plea often made by those who believed social science could not flourish without the application of the natural science method. Stanley Hoffman's plea made as early as more than half a century ago represents such reasoning. He said:

> I would suggest that the first condition of improvement is a clear recognition of the scholar's purpose. His duty is to seek knowledge and understanding for their own sake; and this implies that the main purpose of research should not be "policy-scientism." The fighting of crusades, the desire to advise policy-makers, the scholar's dedication to or international causes can, and even perhaps should be, the occasion, but they should not be the purpose of theoretical research.[88]

Of course, there were similarly influential voices who maintained that a non-normative social science is simply an unattainable. Karl Mannheim, the noted sociologist-historian, argued in this respect:

> ...the [social] observer himself does not stand outside the realm of the irrational, but is a participant in the conflict of forces. This participation inevitably binds him to a partisan view through his evaluations and his interests. Furthermore, and most important, is the fact that not only is a political theorist a participant in the conflict because of his values, and interests, but the particular manner in which the problem presents itself to him, his most general mode of thought including even his categories, are bound up with general political and social undercurrents.[89]

In its pursuit of a normative social "science," however, Mazruiana is not an exception. What is exceptional about Mazruiana may not, therefore, be that it adopts a normatively oriented mode of analysis. Instead, it may be its openness in advocating the greater utility of such orientation in social research. In a 1969 essay, Mazrui argued in favor of a consciously normative social science that, for him, was both a desirable and attainable since, after all, "the applied component of social science is perhaps not a separate factor but simply what emerges when normative theory and scientific theory are conscripted into the service of social policy."[90] In short, Mazruiana is free from the pretension that it is value-free. To this effect, Mazrui asked himself in one of his recent lectures: "Can this story-teller disentangle himself from the story?" And his answer was: "This author has not too sharply separated

Paradigm Lost, Paradigm Regained 53

the participant from the observer in himself."[91]

In more specific terms, Mazrui has also advocated that Afrocentricity ought to be the perspective of choice for Africana studies since it is only this approach that "stands a chance of producing results."[92] In openly advocating a normative social science, Mazruiana affirms its consistency with the position of social constructivism, or the New IR, on this issue— normative concern should inform both the scope and method of a scientific research. As Robert Jervis, the noted scholar of International Relations, put it:

> The normative agenda is...more apparent with social constructivism. The obvious desire is to see world politics transformed by the spread of appropriate norms, identities, and concepts of world politics.[93]

Normative bias is therefore a permissible methodological practice for undertaking a disciplined inquiry within the constructivist framework. In the chapter that follows I shall return to the normative aspects of Mazruiana in the context of its epistemological orientations.

---

1 Lebow (2001: 547); for the opposite view see Forde (1995: 141-160).
2 Nietzsche (1998: 16).
3 Nietzsche (1998: 17).
4 See for instance Ruggie (1998: 855-885).
5 Ruggie (1998: 881-882)
6 Ruggie (1998: 881).
7 Cox (1992: 138).
8 For a discussion of this theme see Wallerstein (1999: 175-176). For a philosophical treatment of Mazruiana in the African/Islamic context see Morewedge (1998: 122-149).
9 Marshall (1992: 14).
10 Porter (1994: 108).
11 Mazrui (2000a: 89).
12 Mazrui (1993: 528).
13 Mazrui (1993a: 529).
14 Mazrui (1973a: 102).
15 Mazrui (1963a: 94).

16 Mazrui (1978: 95).
17 Mazrui (1986a).
18 Mazrui (1986: 28).
19 Mazrui (1986b: 28).
20 Mazrui (1972).
21 Mazrui (1972: 5).
22 Mazrui (2000a: 89).
23 Mazrui (1972: 17).
24 Mazrui (1975a: 11).
25 See for example Markakis (1998).
26 For instance see Philpott (2000: 206-245).
27 Wendt (1999: 31).
28 Wendt (1999: 31).
29 Mazrui (1971).
30 Mazrui (1971: 48).
31 Kelly (1994: 85).
32 Mazrui (1971: 35-36).
33 Mazrui (1977d: 7).
34 Mazrui (1974a: 12).
35 Mazrui (1974a: 3).
36 Rosenau and Durfee (1995: 35).
37 Rosenau and Durfee (1995: 35).
38 Mazrui (1995b: 338).
39 Diamond (1996: 20-37).
40 Mazrui (2000c: 3).
41 Mazrui (2000d: 380).
42 Source: WWW
   publication details unavailable.
43 Mazrui (2000c: 3).
44 Source: WWW
   publication details unavailable.
45 Mazrui (2000d).
46 Huntington (1993: 22-49).
47 Mazrui (1975a: 8-9).
48 Mazrui (1972: 285).
49 Jackson and Sorensen (1999: 114).
50 Jackson and Sorensen (1999: 122).
51 Mazrui (1975a: 9).
52 For discussion see Wells (2000: 116-120).
53 Mazrui (2000e: 362).
54 Mazrui (2000e: 362).
55 Mazrui (2002f: 2). Also see Mazrui (2000e: 23).
56 wendt (1991: 48).

57 Mazrui (1967a)
58 Mazrui (1967a: 238-239).
59 Mazrui (1995a: 23).
60 Mazrui (1995a: 23).
61 Nettl (1968: 561).
62 Weber (1964: 156).
63 Mazrui (1996a: 53).
64 Brown (1999: 531).
65 Strange (1988 : 45, 64, 91, 119).
66 Mazrui (1985a: 181-183).
67 Nye and Owens (1996: 21).
68 Mazrui (1975a: 3).
69 Mazrui (1975a: 3).
70 Mazrui (1975a: 3).
71 Nye and Owens (1996: 21).
72 Mazrui (1975: 4).
73 Mazrui (1975a: 6).
74 Mazrui (1975a: 9).
75 Mazrui (1975a: 8-9).
76 Mazrui (1975a: 8).
77 Mazrui (1975a: 9-11).
78 Mazrui (1975a: 12).
79 Mazrui (1975a: 12).
80 Mazrui (173b: 109); see also chapter six of this book.
81 Mazrui (1993b: 523-524).
82 Mazrui (1993b: 535).
83 Mazrui (1997a: 127).
84 Mazrui (2000c: 2).
85 Mazrui (1996a: 153).
86 Mazrui (1996a: 174).
87 Carr (1990: 23).
88 Hoffman (1959: 349).
89 Mannheim (1960: 4).
90 Mazrui (1969a: 179).
91 Mazrui (200e: 23).
92 Mazrui (1992b: 3).
93 Jervis (1998: 974).

4. Mazruiana Epistemology and Style

Introduction

Writing on Mazruiana, Chaly Sawere asked in 1998 the following question: "...the twentieth century is the most prolific literary century of all time for Africa. In sheer *quantity* Mazrui probably leads the way. However, is there enough *quality* to make him an African immortal?"[1] In relation to Sawere's pertinent question, and subsequent to a closer examination of Mazruiana, I am inclined to answer in the affirmative most emphatically in spite of the fact that in its style Mazruiana is, as Mazrui himself admits, "caught between the formal and the informal, the rigorous and the casual, careful scholarship and polemical argument."[2] As a partial substantiation of my position, I shall proceed with the discussion of the epistemological/methodological issues relating to Mazruiana's notion of how the political world ought to be studied. Then, I shall discuss the style of Mazruiana.

Why Mazrui Writes

I shall begin with the question of why Mazrui writes, or what his motives are, both in the broader and narrower senses of the term. Of course only Mazrui himself could give a definitive answer to the question. In light of the growing interest in his vast intellectual outputs, he will someday hopefully do exactly that. In the meantime, I shall venture to offer a set of tentative answers by organizing my thoughts around the following four possible motivating variables: political purpose, historical impulse, esthetic enthusiasm, and the desire for recognition.[3] Although the priority accorded to each variable might vary depending on the time and subject matter, all of these motives are evident in Mazruiana.

Mazrui writes for something; he writes for someone. Mazruiana is purpose oriented, purpose both in the normative and political senses. Mazruiana in its many forms can be regarded as a polemic in which the ultimate goal is to implant in the reader's mind a point of view or, at least, to set an agenda. Profound as Mazrui's ideas are, he performs the implanting mostly in small doses, in the form of short essays. Although his writings throw light on different aspects of socio-political phenomena, the driving force behind them is not pure research or, as he once put it, "an adventure in abstraction to sharpen the mind."[4] The parallelism between the steadily changing themes of Mazruiana, if not its major concern on the one hand, and the political realities of the times on the other, attests to a strong sense of political purpose in it. As a relative of Mazrui reminisces: "As far back as his Uganda days, Ali Mazrui was asked by President Milton Obote 'Are you sure you know the difference between being a political scientist and being a politician?' President Obote was getting fed up with Mazrui's criticism of Obote's policies, disguised as political science!"[5]

The fact nevertheless remains that there is not such a thing as a value-free political science. The very advocacy of a value-free political science is not itself value-free. Mazruiana's political motives, in the broader sense, seem to overshadow all the other mo-

Paradigm Lost, Paradigm Regained

tives. This kind of impression results in part from Mazruiana's openness about its normative orientations as well as the versatility and sophistication with which they are articulated. Accordingly, Mazrui clarified his position on what he thinks is the place of values in political science: "...political consciousness in the political scientist is prior to his acquisition of either the ethos of scholarship or the specialized skills of his discipline. A political scientist had first to be a politically conscious animal before he could move in the direction of acquiring the necessary equipment from his discipline."[6]

As elaborated in the previous chapter, Mazrui also aspires to present "reality" as he thinks it should be presented. This is the kind of historical impulse that energizes Mazruiana. The very themes and titles of Mazruiana texts bear testimony to such historical impulse. Although historical impulse and political purpose do overlap in certain ways, the former is primarily geared towards the "re-presentation" of "reality" and the latter towards changing it in a desirable way. As a form of social inquiry driven by historical impulse, Mazruiana thus resists attempts to impose hegemony of discourse.

What about the esthetic enthusiasm in Mazruiana? Mazruiana's esthetic attraction is one reason why it is refreshingly readable. Its esthetic qualities, including its elegance and grace and the lucidity of its prose, were evident from the very early writings of Mazrui. Some would argue that over the past few years the quality of Mazruiana has slightly shrunk in this respect. However, what seems truer is that the later Mazruiana texts are as esthetically superb and insightful as the earlier ones although the former tends to be more of synthesis of earlier works and the latter more originally analytical in nature.

Leonard Doob said in his review of one of Mazrui's books: "Versatile, stimulating, sparkling, sophisticated, erudite, perspicacious—select almost any flattering adjective you wish, and it will be applicable in general to this Political Scientist [Ali Mazrui]."[7] Another reviewer by the name of D. A. Low observed: "Ali Mazrui provides...vintage contributions with more elegance to the paragraph than most people contrive to a whole paper..."[8] Likewise the literary sophistication of Mazruiana has long been recognized by many students of Mazruiana and others. As one close observer put it, in Mazruiana, "...one senses not so much a pen writing as a voice pronouncing."[9] The same esthetic aspect of Mazruiana has also at times puzzled others leading some of them to ask whether there is a frustrated novelist in Mazrui the social scientist.[10]

In short, it is crystal clear that the esthetic element is powerfully present in Mazruiana. Mazrui is always mindful about how he says things, if not more than, at least as much as what he says. The precise extent to which esthetic considerations have influenced the development of this body of knowledge is, however, far from clear. I shall discuss in greater detail the style of Mazruiana in a separate section in a short while.

The last motivating variable to be considered is the desire for recognition. How do we know if this variable provides an impetus to a scholarly work? In a field of study where a seemingly detached (or "objective") style of writing is the widely chosen approach, it is hard to readily identify the influence of egoism in intellectual development. But, it must be admitted, this motive is always there to varying degrees behind all scholarly endeavors. No scholar is indifferent to considerations of how his or her intellectual output will be received. Perhaps it can even be argued that an element of egoism is intimately linked to human nature.

If it is true to say that the desire for recognition influences a significant part of intellectual activity, it is even truer to add that such influence is more discernible in some spheres than in others and is more visible at one time and in one person than in another.

Paradigm Lost, Paradigm Regained 61

The presence of such motivating force in Mazruiana is clear, taking its obvious expression in what has been called the semi-autobiographical style of Mazruiana. Such a style is significant in many ways not least because it represents a methodological challenge to positivism so long as it is a consciously "constructionist" activity. The style also confers greater plausibility to the quest for recognition as a significant driving force behind a scholarly work. But, it seems almost certain, that if (substantial part of) Mazruiana had been presented in a style different from that of a semi-autobiography, it would have in the process deprived itself of one of its unique and attractive features. But where does Mazruiana's semi-autobiographical style of political analysis come from? There is no doubt that the origin of Mazrui's interest in autobiographical style does have deeper roots. I shall offer my own hypothesis in regard to this in a moment. Irrespective of its ultimate source, Mazrui has in any case advocated the personalized and semi-autobiographical approach to the study of aspects of political science. He has argued, for instance:

> Because political consciousness is so intricately bound up with the growth of a person's general awareness, political scientists should perhaps devote more time to using their own lives as data for the study of the growth of political consciousness.[11]

Personalized and semi-autobiographical styles have, as I pointed out above, decisive advantages of their own which especially in the case of Mazruiana by far outweigh the disadvantages. Without usage of such a style, Mazruiana might not have received the acclamation it has up to now for the simple reason that far less people would have read it. Because of the uniqueness and rarity of its styles and because of the weight of its ideas, it is conceivable that Mazruiana would recruit greater number of students in the future and that Mazruiana's concise and expressive concepts as well as its grand hypotheses relating to political science and international relations would eventually infiltrate the academic discipline and receive more rigorous scrutiny than they have received so far.

Semi-Autobiographical Style

It has been indicated above that students of Mazruiana have identified an autobiographical or semi-autobiographical style of writing as one distinguishing feature of Mazruiana.[12] This style of writing approaches what Laurel Richardson has called a form of evocative writing, the narrative of the self. Richardson elaborated further what this style of writing entails:

> This is a highly personalized, revealing text in which an author tells stories about his or her own lived experience. Using dramatic recall, strong metaphors, images, characters, unusual phrasings, puns, subtexts, and allusions, the writer constructs a sequence of events, a 'plot,' holding back on interpretation, asking the reader to 'relive' the events emotionally with writer.[13]

That semi-autobiography, or evocative writing understood in the above sense, is one characteristic style of Mazruiana that is obvious. What is not so obvious at first glance is its philosophical foundation. But the obscurity is minimized by what we can learn, directly and indirectly, from Mazruiana itself. First, it is clear that there is a "frustrated novelist" in Mazrui. And novelists are by definition autobiographical even when they are not explicitly so—they use data from their life experiences.[14]

The semi-autobiographical style in Mazruiana seems to have also been solidified at least in part via the influence of similarly autobiographically-oriented political writings Mazrui had read in the early years of his long intellectual journey. The texts Mazrui has mentioned in this regard include Jomo Kenyata's *Facing Mount*

Kenya, M. Kariyuki's, *Mau Mau Detainee*, Kwame Nkrumah's *Ghana: The Autobiography of Kwame Nkrumah*, Tom Mboya's *Freedom and After*, Waruhiu Itote's *'Mau Mau'* General, Karari Njama and Donald Barnett's *Mau Mau from Within*. The names as such do not greatly matter, but Mazrui's critical interest in the form and content of the writings does. In a section of one of his books bearing the subtitle, *Biography and Culture*, Mazrui described Kariuki's book as a work which "[i]n many ways...compares favorably with that political classic of African autobiography, Nkrumah's *Ghana—The Autobiography of Kwame Nkrumah*."[15]

Later on, this semi-autobiographical style appears to have become an important part of the Mazruiana methodology constituting a clearly recognizable deep Mazruiana pattern. In fact Mazrui's interest in the significance of biography as a useful source of data is so deep that early in his professional career he had proposed to write up a biography of Jomo Kenyatta. The response to the offer was nevertheless "a tactful but firm rejection."[16]

Mazrui argued in 1973 that "a political scientist is one who combines political consciousness with effective use of the ethos and the conceptual tools of the discipline and since political consciousness is attained through the life of the individual, it may be profitable for a political scientist to use semi-autobiography both as the source of data and style of analysis."[17] And he has continued to practice what he had preached. But, as I elaborate below, the unique stylistic features of Mazruiana are not limited to semi-autobiography.

Styles of Argument

For my purpose, here I redefine Mazruiana as a discourse on society and culture articulated with a gripping style of presentation. It is a kind of discourse that, even if one chooses to dislike the conclusions, is hard to disagree with the soundness of the analysis that led to the conclusions. Such appealing quality of Mazruiana has to do as much with its style as it has with its substance. In the pages that follow I shall focus on some of the literary devices Mazruiana employs. However, I must admit from the outset that the limits imposed upon me by the narrowness of my field of training prevent me from doing justice to the subject. But the discussion should at least provoke others to do it right.

What is the relationship between a rigorous usage of literary devices and scientific investigation? Some would say that the usage of literary devices is itself a method of inquiry and therefore a part of (social) science. I do not contend with such a perspective. But, for ease of analysis, it is still possible to divide Mazruiana into a science and an art while at the same time allowing a degree of overlap between the two.

For reasons other than the semi-autobiographical style, it is impossible for Mazruiana readers to read more than a few lines of a piece of writing by Mazrui without knowing it is written by him. One of these reasons is that Mazrui does not write in a circular way. His usages of some of the linguistic devices also exhibit certain peculiar features. Mazruiana uses powerfully insightful comparative antithesis in its arguments to produce the desirable effect in the minds of the reader. More often than not, it compares what is almost always incomparable at first glance.

Almost every time one comes across a Mazruiana comparison, the immediate reaction would be such as this: "what do these two (events, people, processes etc.) have in common?" This way of starting an argument also almost always arouses the interest of a serious reader thereby creating an anticipatory desire to read the material through. In virtually all of his writings Mazrui employs this technique incredibly well. For illustrative purposes, I can mention a few of them.

In his *Human Obligation and Global Accountability*, Mazrui wrote the following in the opening pages of his essay: "...Africa helped to produce Columbus, and Columbus in turn helped to produce the United States and Black America."[18] It would seem very likely that even a well-informed reader would be perplexed upon reading the above in the opening page of an essay. But the kind of perplexity that arises is not one that would prompt the reader to close off the book and put it aside, but one which, paradoxically, motivates further reading to see how this scholar would relate two things which are "obviously so unrelated." But upon reading even only a couple of pages, the inquisitive reader would nod in agreement with Mazrui that the two phenomena were indeed related.

Perhaps Omari Kokole has this form of imaginative comparison in mind when he reminded us of Mazrui's power to "x-ray" ideas.[19] At first glance only few would suspect, for example, that Nkrumah shared a striking similarity with Czar and Lenin.[20] Even those who might sense such a similarity are most unlikely to express it in similar terms. Other compelling examples include the postulated link between the impeachment of Warren Hastings and the Nuremberg Trials or European fascism and European imperialism or Bismarck and Hitler,[21] David Livingstone, Albert Schweitzer and Rudyard Kipling,[22] as well as the links between 20th century Uganda and the Holy Roman Empire,[23] the African state and a political refugee,[24] Othello and O. J. Simpson,[25] and the list goes on.

In one of his recent works, Mazrui compared the development of Japan and the underdevelopment of Africa, and "x-rayed" the experience of the two.[26] He then suggested that the logic of the efforts toward development in the countries were the reverse of each other, so they lead to opposite outcomes.[27] Mazrui's usage of analogy and comparison in this way has two principal purposes: clarification and persuasion. His formulations are further enlivened by the skillful use of rhythmic variation. In his essay on soldier Idi Amin and boxer Mohammed Ali, he used the following style of exposition:

> The supremacy of the two individuals in their own domains of excellence and power was almost equally vulnerable. In the field of war, Amin was a gunshot away from either an assassination or a coup. In the field of sport, Muhammed Ali was a bell away from defeat by a rival in the boxing ring. The presidency of Amin and the official and unofficial championship of Muhammad Ali were both subject to sudden termination by either a decisive bullet or a decisive blow on the chin.[28]

Almost in all of his works, Mazrui brilliantly employs in this way imaginative comparison. In some of his works this type of insightful comparison is what the writing is all about, from the beginning to the end.[29] Perhaps it was observation such as this that led one reviewer in *The American Political Science Review* to say:

> From a methodological point of view, Mazrui demonstrates a rare intellectual brilliance. He frequently uses dichotomous schemes of classification which are genuinely original and sometimes surprisingly witty.[30]

The question that arises now is this: how could one develop such a high level of sharpness and sophistication to make this form of penetrating comparative analysis? Such analysis certainly requires, among other things, deep empirical knowledge of and intimate familiarity with subjects across a broad range of fields, the capacity to critically analyze and synthesize this knowledge at the same time and, equally important, the ability to bring literary art into political science. In other words, it takes an artist and scientist to acquire such analytic skill.

In addition, what is required is, as I pointed out in the first chapter, a knowledge which is conveyed not merely through the outer five senses but, and most importantly, knowledge acquired through what John Locke called *reflection*, that is, knowledge conveyed through inner senses.[31] It is not conceivable how without these qualities one would be able to dialectically and artistically relate such things as Nkrumah's style of leadership with that of Czar and Lenin,[32] John Locke and Mahatma Gandhi,[33] the Bolsheviks and the Bantu,[34] the Japanese and Buganda,[35] or Mahatma Gandhi and Karl Marx, and so on.[36]

In his selection of words as well as in the arrangements of incidents and arguments, Mazrui follows a clear and purposeful logic. He often uses a structure of argument that proceeds from general to specific, and arranges his thoughts in order of their importance. A good example of this structure is evident, among the many other works, in the *World Culture and the Black Experience*.[37]

It can therefore be said that one characteristic which makes Mazruiana, to use Rupert Emerson's characterization of Mazrui's work "always enriching as well as entertaining,"[38] is the consistent magnificence and brilliance with which Mazrui puts to use comparison.

Metaphor is another heuristic tool of Mazruiana. Quite early on in his long career, Mazrui asserted :

> Like creative literature, political analysis has to resort at times to the use of analogy and metaphor. The strength of metaphor lies in its transphenomenal comparative utility. It brings forth the associations of one category of life to illuminate a different area of observation.[39]

But what is the place of metaphor in social scientific inquiry? On this question, I concur with the metaphorical answer provided by Laurel Richardson:

...metaphor, is the backbone of social science writing. Like the spine, it bears weight, permits movement, is buried beneath the surface, and links parts together into a functional, coherent whole. As this metaphor about metaphor suggests, the essence of metaphor is the experiencing and understanding of one thing in terms of another. This is accomplished through comparison or analogy.[40]

Mazruiana employs metaphors that are both illuminating and colorful by relating something that is analogous, but not similar to another thing. The kind of metaphors used in Mazruiana are usually "fresh" metaphors rather than conventional or "stored" metaphors, and their ultimate purpose is "to communicate a complex patterned set of properties in a shorthand that is understood by the members of a speech community who share relevant mutual knowledge."[41] Again, one of the many works in which Mazrui brilliantly employs metaphor is *The African State as a Political Refugee*, where he concludes that "the African State can conceivably be a literal refugee and not merely a metaphorical one."[42] Other colorful examples are found in *Exit Visa From the World System: Dilemmas of Cultural and Economic Disengagement*, where he observed:

> The twentieth century has witnessed two forms of international radicalism. One involves a knock from those who are left out in the cold. This is the radical knock of entry—the outsiders are clamoring for the right of participation. The other knock is from those who are already within the system. Some of them may be longstanding inmates; others could be newly admitted into the structure—but have had a culture shock on seeing the inside. This is the radical knock of exit, the urge to leave the system, the perceived imperative of disengagement.[43]

Following a similar style of presentation, Mazrui had once compared the first United Nations Conference on Trade and Development (UNCTAD) to a global trade union after which he aptly added: "[u]nlike the workers in individual countries, however, the poor nations could not really 'go on strike' and hurt the rich countries."[44] Such examples inundate Mazruiana.[45] Mazruiana's uniqueness in this regard lies not so much in its use of metaphor as in the exceptional clarity and effectiveness of the message portrayed through them. He related this in *The African Condition*, a book based on his 1979 BBC Reith Lectures.[46] This book combines rhythmic variation, paradox and metaphors, in an exceptionally elegant way.[47] And anyone who reads Mazrui's other writings will frequently come across similar styles used in a variety of contexts in varied ways.

In his discussion of oratory, Mazrui elsewhere relates the essence and uses of comparative imagery in these terms: "Oratory…need not rest on the orator's verbal originality, but might be even more dependent on styles of using familiar formulations in a new way…An effective use of comparative imagery could help decide a case."[48] It is here that another Mazruiana style that is also related to the above, looms to relevance. This is the style of standing a popular maxim, or a received truth, on its head, and substantiating why the revised way of looking at it is equally plausible, if not more so.

For instance, when he introduced his concept of "shifts in cultural paradigms" in his *The 'Other' as the 'Self' Under Cultural Dependency*, Mazrui's formulation was structured within such a framework of reasoning. In the end, it can be seen that a new dimension was added to the notion of "paradigm shift," originally articulated by Thomas Kuhn. Using the concept of "paradigm shift," Kuhn sought to explain how big scale changes take place in scientific thought. Referring to Kuhn's idea, Mazrui maintained: "…paradigmatic changes are caused not merely by great minds like those of Copernicus, Newton, Darwin, and Einstein, nor only by great social movements like Islam and the Protestant revolution, but also by acculturation and normative diffusion."[49] It is important to note that in pursuing this argument, Mazrui did not aspire to repudiate Kuhn's notion of shifts in scientific paradigms. He only sought to and did add a new dimension to it.

Mazrui also broadened Bertrand Russell's well-known suggestion that "civilization was born out of the pursuit of luxury." In Mazrui's formulation: "…civilization was born out of the pursuit of creative synthesis. The synthesis may be between ethics and knowledge, between religion and science, between one culture and another. The central dynamic is creative synthesis."[50] Further still, the same logic of reasoning was at work in his *Identity Politics and the Nation-State Under Siege: Towards A Theory of Reverse Evolution*.[51] In reference to some of the profound dialectical and cultural changes in the concluding years of the twentieth century, he maintained: "The state may be *'withering away,'* but in a sense which is dramatically different from what either Marx, Engels or Lenin envisaged."[52] In a related way, he observed elsewhere: "When socialist revolutionaries capture the state, it is not the state which starts to wither away—it is socialism itself. The state corrodes socialism—rather than socialism corroding the state."[53] A similar structure of arguments is found in Mazrui's earlier works.[54]

In this way, rhetorical paradoxes are then related in Mazruiana with carefully interwoven themes to offer a universe of perception and cognition; a societal paradigm, a world view. Here is another example: "[s]ocialism in Europe emerged primarily as an ideology of distribution—worrying more about how best to distribute wealth than about how to create it. But socialism in Africa is primarily an ethic of development—the problems of Africa being more those which demand that wealth be created than those which are concerned about 'social justice' in a distributive sense."[55]

In his *The Africans*, too, Mazrui effectively employs the same technique. In one instance, this was how he put it: "Franklin D. Roosevelt once said to Americans, when faced with the economic crisis of the 1930s, 'The only thing we have to fear is fear itself.' For my turn I am tempted to say to fellow Africans, facing a series of severe political, economic, social and cultural crises in the 1980s, 'The main thing we need to change is our own changeability."[56] In *The African State as a Political Refugee*, he reasoned: "George Bernard Shaw used to say that the British and the Americans were a people divided by the same language. It may be truer and more poignant to say that the Somali are people divided by the same culture."[57] Ironic statements have a similarly familiar presence in Mazruiana. For instance, he argued in 1983 that: "Western imperialism opened up Africa to capitalism, but the same imperialism has made Africa increasingly receptive to radical critiques of the world system."[58] In a recent *Foreign Affairs* article, again, he observed:

> Against Western claims that Islamic "fundamentalism" feeds terrorism, one powerful paradox of the twentieth century is often overlooked. While Islam may generate more political violence than Western culture, Western culture generates more street violence than Islam. Islam does indeed produce a disproportionate share of mujahideen, but Western culture produces a disproportionate share of muggers. The largest Muslim city in Africa is Cairo. The largest Westernized city is Johannesburg. Cairo is much more populous than Johannesburg, but street violence is only a fraction of what it is in the South African city.[59]

In another work of his, *European Exploration and Africa's Self-Discovery*, Mazrui combines irony with rhythmic variation: "African nationalism has...been caught between the insult of being unknown and the dignity of being unfamiliar. Nationalists have not been sure whether to be pleased that the European explorers 'revealed' so much, or to be insulted at the presumption that there had been so much to 'reveal.'"[60] In the same vein, in *The Blood of Experience* Mazrui relates the contradictions of contemporary Africa which took the forms of "conflict by too much government versus conflict generated by too little; conflict generated by too many ethnic groups, as distinct from conflict ignited by too few ethnic groups."[61]

Another attraction of Mazrui's style of writing and reasoning, and consequently its appeal even to those with whom he disagrees, is the modesty and great sensibility he shows towards the ideas of others, irrespective of how much he disagrees with them. When he finds a contradiction in the arguments of those who disagree with his lines of thought, Mazrui does not seize upon the opportunity enthusiastically and rush to humiliate them. Instead he carefully presents his thought in a cool-headed manner. As it turns out, this method is also all the more effective. For instance, in *Nkrumah: the Leninist Czar,* a work in which Mazrui discusses the intellectual evolution of Kwame Nkrumah, he clearly follows this approach.[62] Nkrumah's statements Mazrui referred to in the work are contradictory, more so especially when it is realized that Nkrumah expressed those contradictory positions in the same book, *I Speak of Freedom, A Statement of African Ideology*. However, Mazrui did not show excessive eagerness to seize upon the opportunity to dismiss Nkrumah on this point as a confused statesman. Instead Mazrui chose only to indicate that there is a degree of arguability about the compatibility of the two statements by Nkrumah.

A technique such as the above is effective and appealing not only to a neutral-minded reader but even to those who would align themselves with Nkrumah's position. It should perhaps be added that one has to overcome great personal temptation to be able to put one's intellectual opponent in a relatively positive light, especially since it is sometimes assumed that one could not raise his position without stepping on someone else's neck.

For a controversial writer, both the pressure and the temptations are strong for crossing the lines of decorum. It is hard to say how Mazrui was able to overcome these pressures and temptations, especially in view of the fact that he often raises controversial issues and asks controversial questions. There is no doubt the controversial questions he raises are in part intended to arouse the interest of the reader as much as it is to "re-present" history. His conclusions, too, are often as controversial. Yet, except for a few abortive censorships by some publishers and funding organizations, there have not been serious scholarly or political challenges in opposition to what he wrote or said. This is perhaps attributable, at least partially, to Mazrui's skillful ways of articulating his thoughts.

One such device of articulation, which Mazrui seems to have put to use, always effectively, is the rhetorical question. When used properly, this linguistic device functions as a safety valve in approaching a controversial issue. This is not to say that Mazruiana abandons its major theses into air; it does appropriately address the questions it asks. Yet the point is not merely how a controversial issue is settled; it is also how the issue is raised in the first place. The rhetorical question has a moderating effect even on an otherwise infuriating idea. I shall give an example of Mazruiana's usage of this style in a moment.

Mazrui frequently uses opening statements which are always clear, but whose intent is sometimes mysterious and baffling until one reads through. This is at times interwoven with a rhetorical paradox by portraying a reality that is in an apparent contradiction to the one we "know."

A related device, in which the essayist refrains from rounding off his/her writing with a neat final judgment, is called implicative closing, and is usually seen towards the closing of Mazrui's arguments. This strategy allows the essayist to suggest a judgment rather than to formulate one by stopping short, allowing the reader to infer the conclusion.[63] Although Mazrui has continued to this date to use these strategies, it was understandably at the dawn of his career that he indirectly told us the utility of this method for dealing with controversial issues. In *Sacred Suicide*, a chapter in one of his books, Mazrui begins by asking what may be regarded as a rhetorical question: Did Jesus Christ commit suicide? He then opens the paragraph by admitting that this is not a usual type of question:

> A startling question! A question which, to Christians and Muslims alike, verge on blasphemy. Some might even assert that it is blasphemy. But that would be an exaggeration. There is a spiritual impotence in inquiry which saves it from sinning. Only answers have the capacity to blaspheme. And we have yet to answer the question 'Did Jesus Christ commit suicide?'[64]

Sometimes Mazrui's rhetorical questions are disguised assertions. And, at other times, they represent a combination of implicit avowal, or approval as the case may be, and an actual query. In the organization and structure of its arguments Mazruiana employs a clear pattern. It often uses the question and answer transition. In addition to clarity, such a device also adds modesty, however the strength of a claim or conclusion.

Structurally, Mazruiana is loosely defined, that is, a point is developed, left for a moment, to be returned to later, rather than carefully following a pre-stated sequential outline from point to point. This structuring technique seems specially fit for the semi-autobiographical style of Mazruiana. One of the many good examples of the usage of this structure is in *Islam and the End of History*.[65]

Another central feature of Mazruiana is its richness with neologisms and oxymoric combinations that are formed by derivation, by compounding, by gratuitous invention (coinage), or by blending or amalgamation. (See chapter six). In addition to their captivating appeal, the significance of neologisms lies in their simplifying role for representations that are expressed, if they are expressed at all, in other texts only by phrases or clausal description. In this sense, Mazruiana neologisms are not merely new words but they are also the encapsulation of newly formulated ideas. In the concluding chapter of this book, I shall return to some of the issues raised in this chapter and broadly sum up what all this means for situating Mazruiana in the social sciences, especially in relation to its methodological and epistemological orientations.

1 Sawere (1998: 288).
2 Mazrui (1980b: viii).
3 These variables are from Orwell (1981: 312-316).
4 Mazrui (1963a: 122).
5 Alamin Mazrui (2001: 8).
6 Mazrui (1973b: 101).
7 Doob (1968).
8 Low (1972).
9 Kokole (1998: 3).
10 Sawere (1998: 275).
11 Mazrui (1973b: 101).
12 See for example Kokole (1998: 4).
13 Richardson (1994: 521).
14 Interview with Mazrui June 26, 2002 (Binghamton, NY).
15 Mazrui (1972: 28).
16 Mazrui (1976d: 155).
17 Mazrui (1973b: 101).
18 Mazrui (1993a: 30).
19 Kokole (1998 : 12).
20 Mazrui (1967a: 113-134).
21 Mazrui (1993a: 329-347).
22 Mazrui (1991 96-102).
23 Mazrui (1976b: 21).
24 Mazrui (1995c: 21-36).
25 Mazrui (1995f: 1-28).
26 Mazrui (1995b: 340).
27 Mazrui (1995b: 340).

28 Mazrui (1977c: 196).
29 For example see Mazrui (1979).
30 Park (1979: 692).
31 Locke (1997: 120-122).
32 See Mazrui (1967a: 113-134).
33 Mazrui (1967e: 11-26).
34 See Mazrui (1976a: 288-306).
35 Mazrui (1978a).
36 Mazrui (1977e: 179-196).
37 Mazrui (1974: 86-87).
38 Emerson (1967).
39 Mazrui (1972: xiii).
40 Richardson (1994: 519).
41 Glucksburg and Keysar (1993: 422).
42 Mazrui (1995d: 21-22).
43 Mazrui (1981b: 62).
44 Mazrui (1967b: 210).
45 Mazrui (1993c: 5).
46 Mazrui (1980b: 2).
47 Mazrui (1980b).
48 Mazrui (1977a: 65-66).
49 Mazrui (1995a: 340-341).
50 Mazrui (2001a: 1).
51 Mazrui (1999: 5)
52 Mazrui (1999: 5).
53 Mazrui (1996b: 56).
54 See for instance Mazrui (1974a: 105).
55 Mazrui (1967a: 154).
56 Mazrui (1986a: 11).
57 Mazrui (1995c: 27).
58 Mazrui (1983a: 202).
59 Mazrui (1997a: 130); for similar structure of argument see also Mazrui (1995e: 13).
60 Mazrui (1969b: 665).
61 Mazrui (1994a: 32).
62 Mazrui (1967b: 121).
63 Kane (2000: 65).
64 Mazrui (1969: 319).
65 Mazrui (1993b).

5. COMPARATIVE CULTURE AND DEVELOPMENT IN MAZRUIANA PEDAGOGY

Introduction

The celebrated African political scientist and philosopher Ali A. Mazrui has imparted to us an extensive multi-disciplinary and inter-disciplinary work of solid scholarship. It is this body of knowledge which has come to be known as Mazruiana. In relation to Japan, its culture and, above all, its rapid economic development, this chapter critically interrogates the relationship between culture and development as expounded in Mazruiana.[1] The idea that although all cultures are unique in some sense, some are more unique than others, and that Japanese culture falls into the latter category, provides the major premise for this chapter.[2] This chapter also corroborates the difference between Mazruiana and related perspectives in connection with the subject under discussion. This chapter concludes that Africa could and should indeed learn from Japan's developmental experience.

In spite of the vastness of the area Mazruiana covers, or perhaps because of this, it does not dwell on Japan. However, as in virtually all other areas, the ideas articulated in Mazruiana about Japan betray substance, making a closer examination of them a worthwhile endeavor. In reference to Japan in the postwar period and in the period immediately preceding it, Mazrui joined other observers of Japan in maintaining that although after the agony of Hiroshima Japan had shed off its militarism, it had not relinquished its imperialism.[3] Some would of course argue that the tarnishing of the image of postwar Japan was less due to its economic imperialism that took non-military forms than to the lingering shadow of the militarism which preceded it. However that may be, Mazruiana once characterized postwar Japan as a country which replaced the imperial samurai by the businessman, the battalions with the multinational corporations, and the honor-motivated harakiri with profit-motivated business.[4] More than what Japanese external economic behavior meant to the Third World in general, the more complex question which has been systematically considered in Mazruiana related to the potential lessons which Africa could derive from Japan's developmental experience. More specifically, Mazrui's question took such form: What is there in Japanese culture which enabled them to beat Westerners at their own industrial game?[5] I shall discuss and elaborate below on Mazruiana's answers. But first a brief review of the contending explanations of Japan's remarkable economic transformation.

Explaining the Japanese "Miracle"

Explanations abound about the rapid economic development of Japan.[6] For all their variegated orientations, these explanations rightly recognize the spectacular speed with which the country achieved industrial success. When it comes to the identification of the most important factors, or the relative importance of individual factors in the process of industrialization, explanations start to take different, sometimes opposing, paths. Although no school of thought attributes Japanese success to a single variable exclusively, it is possible, at the risk of some oversimplification, to classify the contending theories in light of the factors that are implicitly or explicitly stressed. The materialist school holds the view that Japan's economic success was driven by the felt-need of overcoming the material shortage in the society. Under the circumstances, Japanese were left with one and only one choice: to work harder and organize their society better. This situation also conditioned Japanese to set their goal clearly and pursue its achievement aggressively.[7]

Others link the rapid economic development of Japan to cultural factors. If the severity of material shortage had been the primary driving force of economic development, the argument goes, some of the states now considered to be least developed would have themselves become developmental models. This school insists therefore that Japanese economic success was propelled by cultural attributes unique to Japan, attributes which shaped and underpinned, among other things, attitudes toward work.[8] Apart from this, another way of looking at Japan's economic transformation is based on the domestic/international dichotomy. One group of analysts attribute this transformation to a combination of material and cultural variables.[9] Another group maintains that if it had not been for the favorable postwar international political and economic climate, domestic features of Japan might have made little difference to the nation's economic endeavor. Still for others, it was the combined interplay of all of the above factors which made the Japanese miracle possible.[10]

Mazruiana explains Japan's economic development and industrialization mostly in cultural terms. In fact, for Mazrui, the most fundamental question ought not to be whether culture explains Japan's development or not. Instead it must be: what was there in their culture…which enabled them to remain so Japanese culturally and still pull off an industrial miracle? How did culture as identity and culture as production converge?[11]

Mazrui classifies the industrialization of Japan into two phases.

The first phase was completed after the Meiji restoration of 1868 when "they embarked on a crusade of selective industrialization and technological change under the slogan of 'Western techniques, Japanese spirit.'" The second phase began after the Second World War. This phase was "less culturally selective than the first, but even more technologically triumphant."[12]

Let us return to the major concern of this paper which is about the specific role of culture in the economic transformation of Japan. In his 1990 book, *Cultural Forces in World Politics*, Mazrui offered a functional definition of culture, maintaining that culture serves seven major functions—namely, it provides lenses of perception and cognition, motives for human behavior, criteria of evaluation, a basis of identity, a mode of communication, a basis of stratification, and a system of production and consumption.[13] Elsewhere Mazrui saw the process of acculturation as centering either on values or techniques with a different level of intensity.[14] On closer inspection, Mazrui's functional definition of culture represents the sum of religious, linguistic, racial, aesthetic, moral and normative givens in a society on the basis of which a certain behavioral pattern could be expected. For my present purpose, I single out from Mazrui's definition only language and religion as forms of cultural expressions. I shall return to some of the remaining components of culture later on in the discussion.

Mazrui saw language and religion as having played a significant role in the economic development of Japan and underdevelopment of Buganda in Africa. On the role of language in industrial take off, he argued that capitalism had succeeded best where the language of the marketplace had not been too far removed from the language of the classroom and that in Africa [in contrast to Japan] the language of the marketplace (usually indigenous) and the language of the classroom (usually foreign) were indeed distant.[15]

For illustrative purposes, Mazrui then contrasted the Japanese with the Buganda, one of the tribes in Uganda which had significantly

Paradigm Lost, Paradigm Regained

internalized the influence of "modernization." His conclusion was that "…the Japanese borrowed more techniques than values from the West, while the Buganda borrowed more values than techniques from the West."[16] This is attributable, Mazrui argued, to "[t]he fact that the Japanese undertook their modernization primarily through the Japanese language, and did not become linguistic converts to an alien idiom…"[17] On religion Mazrui maintained that unlike the Japanese, the Buganda embraced Christianity with "a deep sense of inner response" and that "the Christianization of Buganda must therefore be counted as a critical additional level of difference in acculturation between the Ganda and the Japanese."[18]

A methodological question may be raised here about Mazruiana's comparison of the Japanese with the Buganda in relation to the variations in the level of their modernization and westernization, and the comparability of a small tribe, such as Buganda, and a relatively large country, Japan. Even if it is appropriate to compare the two, a critic may insist on asking how the experience of Buganda can be extrapolated to Africa as a whole without falling into the trap of what logicians call an ecological fallacy—the fallacy of extrapolating a generalization from a lower level of analysis to a higher one. In what seems to be an obvious anticipation of the likelihood of such a methodological challenge, Mazrui clarified the values of a result of a comparative analysis of Buganda and Japan. He did this in one of his earlier works where he discussed what he called the *methodology of hypothesizing*. He argued: "comparative politics as a whole means nothing if it does not include readiness to use evidence from one part of Africa as potential material for formulating Africa-wide hypothesis. It would then be up to other researchers to test some of these hypotheses against empirical findings elsewhere in the continent."[19]

Apart from language and religion, according to Mazrui, Japan's ability to acquire Western tools without succumbing to Western subjugation[20] had also to do with the relatively greater power the Japanese retained for defining the course of their own development, especially in relation to the capacity "to transform the educational system, and to choose the relevant forms of indoctrination to accompany the transmission of the new skills."[21] Let us now zoom our observational lens in further on the Japanese culture in order to formulate a cultural hypothesis about the rapid economic transformation of Japan.

Flexibility in Japanese Culture

Many observers of Japanese society and culture note that flexibility defines the nation's system of thought.[22] By cultural flexibility, what is generally meant is the proclivity and versatility "to change in response to the needs of the times, rather than stubbornly clinging on."[23] Here is where the issue of imitation also enters the discussion. It is evidently clear that Japanese place high premium on imitation and this is, as Mazrui also noted, "not new to Japan."[24]

Japanese are also excellent modifiers of what has been imitated. They are adept at making a borrowed technical device or philosophical idea fit the needs of their society.[25] This form of creative imitation has indeed a deep philosophical and cultural tradition, a tradition in which the distinction between imitation and creation is often blurred.[26] In this way, it seems, such creative imitation provided a foundation separating the Japanese not only from Buganda but also from other cultures as well. Mazrui has also argued that "modernization becomes to some extent a readiness to applaud inventiveness, a readiness to encourage discovery."[27] If this is so, we can therefore say that Japan had the cultural ingredients of modernity in place even before it aggressively began to learn from the West.

In the same vein, the cultural givens of the society distinguish Japanese "capitalism" from that of the West, working as the former does in ways neither Adam Smith nor Karl Marx would have understood. One way of illustrating this may be to compare and contrast the

Paradigm Lost, Paradigm Regained

ideas of Adam Smith and Shosan Suzuki.[28] The ideas of these great minds seem to be at the operational center of the mode of capitalist systems in the West and in Japan respectively.

One of the distinguishing features of the idea of Adam Smith is the deep suspicion with which merchants and manufacturers are viewed. In Smith's own well-known words, "It is not from the benevolence of the butcher, the brewer, or the baker, that we expect our dinner, but from their regard to their own interest. We address ourselves not to their humanity, but to their self-love, and never talk to them of our necessities but of their advantage."[29]

On the other hand, a radically different view was articulated by Shosan Suzuki, a Zen monk who lived in the 19th century Japan. Suzuki is regarded by many as a man who laid down a philosophical basis for the development of "capitalism" in Japan. In contrast to Adam Smith, Suzuki made a successful attempt to morally justify a "worldly activity." He wrote: "All is for the good of the world...The all encompassing Buddha-nature manifests in us all works for the world's good; without artisans, such as the blacksmith, there would be no tools; without officials there would be no order; without farmers there would be no food; without merchants, we would suffer inconvenience. All the other occupations as well are for the good of the world."[30] In fact, Suzuki went as far as to assert: "Commerce is the function Heaven has assigned to those whose job is to promote freedom throughout the country."[31]

One conclusion that can be drawn is, therefore, that the Japanese belief-system in this respect is fundamentally different from that of others'. The place of religion in Japan's system of thought, and the effect of this on the nation's rapid industrialization, also reveals a similarly fundamental difference. Writing on the ways in which religion and capitalism compliment each other in Japan, Takeo Kuwabara argued: "Over all Japan's myriad gods and deities, there is no single Allah or Jehovah, no monopolistic god that devours all the others. One all-powerful god would not permit constant shifting from one thing to another. For Japanese, one all-knowing god would be constricting...As it is none of Japan's thousands of gods has too much power. As the old maxim goes, 'If one god throws you, another god will pick you up'...I believe that the absence of an almighty God was an instrumental in [Japan's] success."[32]

At least insofar as the instrumentality of religious values is assumed in this way to be crucial for economic success, Max Weber's argument bears a striking similarity to that of Takeo Kuwabara. However, there is also a sense in which Kuwabara's thesis could be viewed as the Weberian theory *in reverse*. Referring to the difference in the attitudes of different religions toward economic life, Max Weber's quote from his famous book, *The Protestant Ethic and the Spirit of Capitalism*, is a succinct characterization by a contemporary writer reminding us that "the Protestant prefers to eat well, the Catholic to sleep undisturbed." [33] While Weber viewed Protestantism as fostering economic development by inculcating favorable values in the minds of the people, Kuwabara believed commitment to any particular religion is restrictive and undermines flexibility. It is in this way that success in attaining worldly "good" is stressed in Japanese culture and philosophy.

The African Condition: A Mazruiana Diagnosis

Before I return to the general discussion of what Africa could learn from Japan's developmental experience, it may be useful to remind ourselves once again that in Mazruiana, Japan's economic transformation is attributable mainly to its culture, and its ability to absorb western skills. Intricately related to this is also the sense of social duty which binds the Japanese's "self," including their tendency to teach themselves rather than to import expatriates, and to improvise foreign products or make the products by themselves, rather than to try their best to use the imported items.[34] Underlying all of these efforts is a culture that rewards excellence.[35]

That Africa's attempt to modernize has been a dismal failure is a fact.[36] However this is not in the least attributable to the lack of ideas and models. A variety of ideologies ranging from Marxism-Leninism and African socialism to liberal capitalism all failed to produce a tangible result in Africa. As Mazrui put it, "Just as Black Africa had once been the virgin territory for the spread of the Christian Gospel, so it was later to be regarded as virgin area for experiments in developmentalism and modernization theories."[37]

Mazrui explained the reason why these developmental ideas failed to take root in Africa, mainly in terms of the unfavorable nature of the socio-cultural climate in Africa. This is manifested, among other things, in the predisposition towards pursuing prestige rather than profit, consumption rather than production. In short, Mazrui concluded, capitalism came to Africa without "the Protestant ethic."[38] Mazrui attributed Africa's dismal failure in its attempt to modernize to three anomalies - anomalies which can be simultaneously considered to be the causes and consequences of the African condition. These anomalies included: 1) urbanization without industrialization; 2) secularization without scientification 3) capitalism without entrepreneurship.[39]

The question now becomes whether Africa can learn, or imitate Japan in the way the latter imitated the West. A step towards an answer can be taken first by supplying a broad theoretical context for our discussion.[40] Liberalism and Marxism are the two broad categories of theories that purport to explain the political economy of North-South relations. The variants of Marxism include dependency theory and world systems analysis. Liberalism encompasses, in its extreme form, what I shall call the new culturalism.

Without being a monolithic whole, each of these theories has certain distinguishing features of its own. Dependency school stressed that the development of the North was based on the underdevelopment of the South and as such perpetuated the status quo in the interest of the North.⁴¹ Adherents of the world systems analysis underlined that unequal exchange between the core and the periphery led to the perpetual impoverishment of the former but, for them, structural and systemic factors such as the axial division of labor were more relevant.⁴²

On the other side of the theoretical spectrum, liberals explain the underdevelopment of the South in terms of comparative advantage of nations and regions. For them, the North was well-endowed with the factors of production and, therefore, was able to fare better in the global economy. Moreover, liberals point out, regions that were not doing well at any given time could be in a better position in the future provided they adopted proper policies and made efficient use of their comparative advantage, especially the form of comparative advantage that is man-made as opposed to the comparative advantage of mother nature.⁴³

New culturalists, on the other hand, while subscribing to the liberal principle in the broadest sense, emphasized the *decisive* importance of cultural factors for economic development and suggested that there was little that could be done to help certain regions of the world undertake sustainable development. The aforementioned perspectives also diverged with respect to what they regard as the key actors in the international political economy, what they perceived to be the primary concern of their focus, and their domain and core concepts. Needless to say, many of the leading propositions of these approaches significantly reflected the values and agenda of the analysts, thus making it hard for a researcher to employ them for a serious empirical study.⁴⁴

As indicated above, one approach that may be regarded as contrasting with liberalism as a framework for analyzing North-South relations is the world systems analysis.⁴⁵ Both for what it espouses and what it rejects, this approach has greater relevance to the theme of our discussion.

The underlying assumption of the world systems approach is the existence of one global economy. This one world scale economy is progressively more global in scope, has a single or axial division, and has an integration of labor processes both organized and paralleled by a single set of accumulation process between its always more advanced, historically enlarging and geographically shifting core, and its always less advanced, disproportionately enlarging, and geographically shifting periphery.[46]

Also central to world systems analysis are the concepts of core and periphery. They designate different economic zones of the world capitalist economy and are based on a single overarching division of labor. In the modern world system the periphery is the producer of primary products and the core produces secondary products. However, "this is incidental, not essential, to the conception of the core-periphery division of labor, which is a division among integrated production processes, not among particular products."[47]

The world systems perspective significantly departs from other modes of inquiry in its assertion that "the unit of analysis is the world system defined in terms of economic processes and links, and not any unit defined in terms of any juridical, political, cultural, geological, or other criteria."[48] From the world systems perspective, the question of whether or not Africa should or could imitate or learn from the other regions is irrelevant because of the decisiveness of systemic factors and the deepening of the international division of labor.[49]

Less integrated approaches to the North-South issues reflect similarly divergent views when it comes to the issue of the desirability and the possibility of imitating Japan. One view is that Japan could serve as a model for Africa both in respect to the future education and the quest for modern development.[50] The other view advances the contrasting view that African policy makers must look inward because African problems are distinct from Europe, the US, China or Japan.[51]

There is another school of thought, referred to above as the new culturalism, whose growing popularity is partly derived from the emergence of high performing economies of East Asia. Culture is at the center of this emerging orthodoxy on economic development. For this school, no matter what, societies that do not exhibit certain cultural characteristics are less likely to do well and effectively compete in the global economy.[52] But despite the apparent emphasis on culture in Mazruiana as well as in new culturalism, the two schools of thought are, as I elaborate below, clearly distinguishable.

Mazruiana and the New Culturalism

Mazruiana significantly differs from the new culturalism. The former also, of course, recognizes culture's role in economic development. On the other hand, the latter conception of culture is so deterministic to the extent of appropriating the old view that certain cultures, because of their intrinsic features, are damned to backwardness and poverty unlike others which are congenial for progress and the creation of wealth. Such a conception has indeed a long historical root.[53] The scientifically-informed study of culture in the sense expounded in Mazruiana may thus be called cuturology,[54] while the ideologically-driven, post-facto conclusions about the consequences of variations among cultures may be called culturalism.

In 1968 Mazrui demonstrated that the system of analyzing and classifying nations on the basis of the stages of modernization reached had a long-standing historical root.[55] When Mazrui articulated his position, the political development approach, although still dominant, was under attack from different angles. About four decades later there is evident reemergence of what resembles a tradition of analysis which Mazrui was trying to challenge. However, important distinction can be drawn between the old and the new culturalism.

The new culturalism is more sophisticated than the old one, although both share an essentially similar view towards the less industrialized areas of the world. The old culturalists had at least assumed that, along with other measures, institution-building could lead to democracy and development in non-Western societies. On the other hand, the new culturalism does not entertain such an "optimistic" vision since one of its major premises is that the degree to which the ability to create institutions and run them effectively is itself culture-bound.[56] Owing to the increased quantity and quality of anthropological and sociological research, the new culturalism has more of the flavor and tone of a scientific "truth." Yet in the new culturalism, it is not just the Western culture, although it is still at the center, which is portrayed as superior to "other" cultures. Cultures of areas which have managed to industrialize, despite (according to some) or because of (according to others) their being non-Western, are included.

The international context within which the old and the new culturalism emerged also differed significantly. When the old school flourished, decolonization was by and large complete and nationalism was on the rise. Because of the East-West rivalry, so-called Third World countries had at the time some international leverage. Thus Kwame Nkrumah, the first leader of post-independence Ghana, could for example say to his official audience in the US: "I am appealing to the democracies of Britain and the United States for assistance in the first place, but that if this should not be forthcoming, I would be forced to turn elsewhere."[57] But the disintegration of the Communist bloc deprived these countries even of this modest leverage, beginning in the 1990s, and this period, not surprisingly, coincided with the assertive re-mergence of culturalism, the new culturalism.

The 1990s saw the appearance of a number of "scholarly" works which approach development from the perspective of the new culturalism.[58] For my purpose here, I shall nevertheless focus only on Francis Fukuyama's work, *Trust: The Social Virtues and the Creation of Prosperity*.[59] The main thrust of *Trust* was that the most important lesson we could learn from an examination of economic life is that a nation's well-being, as well as its ability to compete, is conditioned by a single, pervasive cultural characteristic: the level of trust inherent in one society.[60]

Pursuing Fukuyama's line of argument, one ultimately reaches the conclusion that the future of less industrialized regions of the world is at best gloomy because they represent an area where lack of trust prevails. This interpretation is reinforced by Fukuyama's assertion that "…a strong and stable family structure cannot be legislated into existence [in the same way] as governments can create a central bank or an army."[61] Immanuel Wallerstein had once argued that "…poor people try to socialize themselves to their situation of poverty."[62] This form of state of consciousness seems in important ways to be also a result of the powerful messages imparted to the poor from the other side. What Fukuyama did in his book was, in effect, to strongly remind "backward" societies, or in his own terminology, "low-trust" societies, that they are not only poor, but they are also doomed to be so, and that their behavioral disposition which made them so backward is culturally-determined.

The sophistication of the new culturalism cannot, however, obscure the internal flaws which undermine its cogency, especially the empirical and logical flaws in it. Comparing North Korea and South Korea, the former East Germany and West Germany, or Taiwan and mainland China during the Cold War years, one can easily grasp the greater relevance of ideas/policies in affecting socio-economic development. Despite the cultural similarity between these pairs of states, there is/was much disparity in the levels of their socio-economic development. The inescapable conclusion that can be drawn here is that misguided policies rather than culture seems to explain the socio-economic performance in these countries.

The direction of the postulated causal link between culture or, more specifically, trust and economic development, is also open to question. The linkage apparently forms the fundamental premise on which the above thesis about trust is based. Certain rival hypotheses nevertheless remain unexamined in the thesis, such as whether or not the level of wealth does also affect the level of trust in a society, rather than the other way round; or whether or not a different conclusion can be reached by undertaking a more comprehensive study of societies across time and culture rather than by a selective *post hoc* reading of a few cases. It could also be the case that even if the relationship between the two variables—trust and economic development—holds, it will not necessarily be linear. It is possible that wealth could affect the level of trust in a given society only up to a certain point after which it could begin to yield a diminishing return.

In addition to the differences indicated above, Mazruiana distanced itself from the new culturalism by answering in the affirmative to the question of whether Africa should imitate (learn from) the experience of other societies, including Japan. As Mazrui himself put it,

> Africa has been studying Western culture for decades in the hope of stimulating its development. It is time that Africa diversifies the cultural models it examines for developmental lessons. Such diversification may help reduce Africa's dependency upon the West in other areas of endeavor as well.[63]

Learning How to Learn

Then what, exactly, can Africa learn from Japan's developmental experience? Mazrui has indirectly addressed this question and explored related issues by comparing, as indicated earlier, Japanese modernization with that of Baganda.[64] The basis for choosing Japan as a subject of comparison is obvious. Baganda was selected as one unit in the pair of comparison because it was, like the Japanese, "particularly successful in responding to the West while remaining deeply loyal to a traditional self."[65]

Using the methodology of causal investigation, Mazrui examined why the Japanese succeeded when the Baganda failed in their developmental efforts, despite the fact that both exhibited "what appears to be a vigorous response to modernization without a total rejection of tradition."[66] In comparing the two, Mazrui sought to identify the possible causes that were missing in one case and present in the other. He discovered three sets of important differences that caused and reflected the difference in the levels and forms of acculturation by the Baganda and the Japanese. These factors included colonization, language, and religion. And then he concluded: "Japan responded to *technical* assimilation before she imbibed *value* acculturation. Baganda reversed the order, as she fell under the spell of Christianity and British tradition of education."[67] In addition, he observed, "in Japan the *samurai* tradition linked deference to discipline quite firmly—and transferred both to the factory and the task of development. In Baganda the contractual culture and its attendant demilitarization helped the Baganda to retain deference without acquiring discipline. Whatever *samurai* elements there might have been in the traditional marital culture of Baganda died with the 1900 Agreement."[68]

As indicated earlier, from a Mazruiana perspective culture influences economic development. However, Mazrui is not for the indiscriminate imitation of foreign culture. He clarified this position as follows:

> First, not all of Africa's problems require a culture change; sometimes, it may just require greater attention to African culture than we have done before. Second, culture change need not take too long when it is required.[69]

Mazrui's first proposition is far less contentious. However, the second one is open to challenge on the grounds that culture change does seem to take longer than he suggested. In this respect, Japanese culture may indeed be misleading as a model since there seems to be elements in Japanese culture which pertain peculiarly to the relatively

Paradigm Lost, Paradigm Regained 93

high speed with which culture changes are affected. One such Japanese cultural feature that seems to have contributed to "the Japanese miracle" is the spectacular receptiveness to foreign ideas, or as we called it above, *creative imitation*. The other accompanying feature is flexibility—the disposition to swiftly adjust to changed circumstances.[70]

Even though it is beyond the scope of my principal concern here, it is also important to note that these very cultural factors have continued to influence Japan's external behavior as well. It can be argued that cultural flexibility helped the transformation of Japan in a relatively short period of time from being a militarist state to a "peace-loving" state, enabling them the Japanese to shift gears swiftly when the situation so required. And behind these elements of culture—i.e., imitation and flexibility— lies the philosophical foundation of the Japanese mode of behavior. As for the essence of this foundation, we can take a hint from Takeo Kuwabara's observation:

> A society such as Japan's, where abstract principles for their own sake are not particularly respected, does not encourage determination that enables one to stick to a position no matter what the circumstances. The principle that matters most is the principle of adjustment and accommodation. Whether it is based on intellectual or emotional response, this is what underlies the art of living, as nature demonstrates in the life patterns of all creatures. Thus at the source of Japanese thought and behavior, instead of abstract universals, we find a type of practical naturalism that emphasizes life itself, and as the basis for action, we find accommodation to changing situations. [71]

It appears to be the case, therefore, that the failures and the achievements of Japan emanated in large part from this kind of deep-rooted system of thought, and that the inadequate attention paid to such notions in Africa's own culture became the vehicle for bringing about the realities of the present-day. What this suggests is of course not that Africa could not and should not try to learn from Japan. Whereas it is desirable to emulate certain cultural aspects that have significantly contributed to the development of "other" societies, it is nevertheless of less use and even detrimental to relish in the culture of others while depreciating one's own. That is why one has to heed the Mazruiana caveat stated above that "...not all of Africa's problems require a culture change; sometimes, it may just require greater attention to African culture than we have given before." [72]

Conclusion

Cultures influence the pace and pattern of economic and political development. But they do not play *the* decisive role in the process. Mazruiana teaches that what Africa must do is not merely try to copy the cultures of others, but also pay due attention to its own culture. The developmental experience of Japan is relevant to Africa both for emulation and stimulation purposes, especially since there are certain African cultural traditions which are clearly evident in Japanese culture. It would therefore be profitable to systematically identify such areas in which Africa can draw upon its own culture and at the same time learn how to better utilize it.

---

1 The claim about the rapidity of Japan's economic development should not obscure the fact that there had been a solid cultural and material foundation that were in place long before the so called the Japanese miracle unfolded.
2 For a sharp critique of the idea of 'the uniqueness' of the Japanese culture, see Peter Dale, *The Myth of Japanese Uniqueness*, London & Sydney: Croom helm, 1986.
3 Ali A. Mazrui, *The Barrel of the Gun and the Barrel of Oil in North –South Equation*, World Orders Model Project, Working paper No.5, New York: Institute for World Orders, 1978, p. 7.
4 Ibid.
5 Ali A. Mazrui, "The African Renaissance: A Triple Legacy of Skills, Values and Gender", A Public Lecture delivered at the National Theatre, Iganmu, Lagos, 26 June 2000, p. 9.
6 For summary of a variety of explanations slightly different from what is presented here, see E. W. Nafziger, *Learning from the Japanese: Japan's Pre-war development and the Third World*, Armong, NY and London: M. E. Sharpe, 1995, pp. 5-10.

Paradigm Lost, Paradigm Regained 95

7 Kenichi Ohmae, *The Mind of the Strategist: The Art of the Japanese Business*, New York: McGraw-Hill, Inc., 1982, especially see pps. 215-241.
8 In this vein, E. Alegre for instance argued: "The industrialization of Japan cannot be repeated in any other countries since the cultural factors at work in Japan and those in other countries are quite dissimilar." See, E. Alegre, "The Modernization of Japan and Its Limits" in Japan and The Japanese, Compiled by The Mainichi Newspapers, Tokyo & San Francisco, Japan Publications Inc.., 1973, pp. 128-129
9 For an analysis which carefully interweaves economic and cultural variables see for example, J. A. J. Hoebe, "Social Bases for Economic Growth", *Japan and The Japanese*, Compiled by The Mainichi Newspapers, Tokyo & San Francisco, Japan Publications Inc.., 1973, pps. 52-72.
10 For example see Lee K. Choy, *Japan: Between Myth and Reality*, Singapore: World Scientific, 1995, specially, pps. 155-184.
11 Mazrui, "The African Renaissance", p. 9.
12 Ibid.
13 Ali A. Mazrui, *Cultural Forces in World Politics*, Oxford: James Currey, 1990, pp. 7-8. These functions of culture are further elaborated in Ali A. Mazrui, *The Social Dimension of Culture and Contemporary Expressions*, Lecture delivered at a Workshop on Culture in Sustainable Development. Investing in Cultural and Natural Endowement. Sponsored by the World Bank and UNESCO, September 28-29, 1998, pp. 1-2.
14 Ali A. Mazrui, *Political Values and the Educated Class in Africa*, Berkeley and Los Angeles: University of California Press, 1978, p. 32.
15 Ali A. Mazrui and Alamin Mazrui, *The Power of Babel: Language and Governance in the African Experience*, Oxford: James Currey, 1998, p. 199.
16 Mazrui, *Political values and the Educated Class in Africa*, p. 32.
17 Ibid., p. 33.
18 Ibid., pp. 33-34.
19 Ali A. Mazrui, "Soldiers as Traditionalizers: Military Rule and the Re-Africanizing of Africa," *Journal of Asian and African Studies*, vol. 12, no. 1-4, p. 236. .
20 Ali A. Mazrui, *The Africans: A Triple Heritage*, Boston and Toronto: Little Brown & Co., 1986, p. 14.
21 Mazrui, *Political Values and the Educated Class in Africa*, p. 33.
22 This is what Ruth Benedict has called 'an ethic of alternatives' or, in the words of Kuwabara takeo, 'the principle of adjustment and accommodation'. See, respectively, Ruth Benedict, *The Chrysanthemum and the Sword: Patterns of the Japanese Culture*, Tokyo: Charles E. Tuttle, 1993 [First published in 1972], p. 304; and Kuwabara Takeo, *Japan and Western Civilizations: Essays on Comparative Culture*, Tokyo: The University of Tokyo Press, 1983, 173.
23 Takeo, *Japan and Western Civilizations*, 1983, p. 80.
24 Ali A. Mazrui, "The Baganda and the Japanese: Comparative Response to Modernization", *Kenya Historical Review*, vol. 4, no. 2, 1976, p. 172. For a dramatic representation of the Japanese love for imitation see J. Tobin, *Re-Made in Japan: Everyday Life and Consumer Taste in a Changing Society*, New Haven: Yale University Press, 1992, p. 3. It is quite

interesting to note here that, although not exactly same sense and connotation, Africans had been described in the past as being "intellectually devoid of the possibilities of ultimate originality" but " endowed with a significant imitative genius." See,Ali A. Mazrui, "'Progress': Illegitimate Child of Judeo-Christian Universalism and Western Ethnocentrism-A Third World Critique", in L. Marx and B. Mazlish (ed.), *Progress: Fact or Illusion?* Ann Arbor: The University of Michigan Press, 1996, p. 163-64.

25 An example of a foreign idea that had been modified to fit domestic purpose is Confucianism with a shifted emphasis on loyalty rather than benevolence as it was conceived by Confucius. For a useful discussion on this subject see M. Morishima, *Why Japanese Succeeded Western Technology and the Japanese Ethos*, Cambridge: Cambridge University Press, 1982, p. 6.

26 N. Honna and B. Hoffer, *An English Dictionary of Japanese Way of Thinking*, Tokyo: Yuhikaku, 1989, p. 148. For a view that Japan is not all imitation see Kenichi Ohmae's, *The Mind of the Strategist: The Art of Japanese Business*, New York: McGraw-Hill, 1982. especially, p. xi.

27 Ali A. Mazrui,, *Africa between the Meiji Restoration And the Legacy of Ataturk: Comparative Dilemmas of Modernization*, Ankara: TISA Matabaacilik Sanayl Ltd., 1984, p. 391.

28 The material consulted on Adam Smith is his, *An Inquiry into the Nature and Causes of the Wealth of Nations*, edited by K. Sutherland, Oxford, New York: Oxford University Press, 1993. A general introduction to the ideas of Shosan Suzuki is found in A. Braverman, *Warrior of the Zen: The Diamond-hard Wisdom mind of Suzuki Shosan*, New York, Tokyo, London: Kodansha International, 1994.

29 Adam Smith *An Inquiry into the Nature and Causes of the Wealth of Nations*, edited by K. Sutherland, Oxford, New York: Oxford University Press, 1993, p. 22.

30 Y. Shichihei, *The Spirit of Japanese Capitalism and Selected Essays*, Trans. By L. Riggs and T. manabu, Lanham: Madison Books, 1992, p. 83.

31 Ibid.

32 Kuwabara, *Japan and Western Civilization*, 1983, p. 82.

33 Max Weber, *The Protestant Ethic and the Spirit of capitalism*, Trans. By T. Parsons, New York: Charles Scribner's Sons, 1958, p. 30.

34 D. Landes, "Culture Make Almost All the Difference", in L. Harrison and S. Huntington (eds.), *Culture Matters: How Values Shape Human Progress*, New York: basic Books, 2000, p. 2.

35 In this connection it may be relevant to refer to what Ore and Sako observed: "...the Japanese do tend to feel that competence is a moral duty and not just a means of earning money by giving satisfaction and that sloppiness is a sin and not just something to avoid because it puts you in danger of getting the sack." See Ronald P. Ore and Mari Sako, *How the Japanese Learn to Work*, London and New York: Routledge, 1989, p. xi.

36 This is a recurrent theme in Mazruiana. The works in which he addresses this theme, especially in relation to culture, include his: "The Political Economy of Nationhood and the Political Economy of the State" in *Millennium: Journal of International Studies* vol. 12, no. 3, 1983, pp. 201-210; Ali A. Mazrui, *Africa between the Meiji restoration And the Legacy of Ataturk: Comparative Dilemmas of Modernization*, Ankara: TISA Matabaacilik Sanayl Ltd.,

1984. ; "Perspective: The Muse of Modernity and the Quest for Development", in P. G. Altbach and S. M. Hassan (ed.), *The Muse of Modernity: Essays on Culture as Development in Africa*, Trenton, NJ and Asmara: Africa World Press, 1996, pp. 1-18; "Africa and the Search for a New International Technological Order", in P. Ndegwa, L. Mureiti and R. Green (eds.), *Development Options for Africa*, Nairobi: Oxford University Press, 1985, pp. 177-185; "The African Renaissance: A Triple Legacy of Skills, Values and Gender", A Public Lecture delivered at the National Theatre, Iganmu, Lagos, 26 June 2000; "Africa between Ideology and Technology: Two Frustrated Forces of Change", in G. M. Carter and P. O'Meara (eds.), *African Independence: The First Twenty-Five Years*, Bloomington: Indiana University Press, 1985, 275-300; "Africa Entrapped: Between the Protestant Ethic and the Legacy of Westphalia", in H. Bull and A. Watson (eds.), *The Expansion of International Society*, Oxford: Clarendon Press, 1984, pp. 289-308..

37 Mazrui, '"Progress", p. 157.

38 Ali A. Mazrui, "Ideology and African Political culture", in T. Kiros (ed.), *Explorations in African political Thought*, New York, London: Routledge, 2001, pp. 115-118.

39 Mazrui, *Africa between the Meiji Restoration And the Legacy of Ataturk*, pp. 386-388.

40 One of the works in which Ali A. Mazrui touches upon the broader theoretical issues in North-South relations include: Ali A. Mazrui, "Technology, International Stratification and the Politics of Growth", *International Political Science Review*, vol.1, no.1, 1980, pp. 63-79.

41 D. Santos, 'The Crises of Development Theory and the Problem of Dependence in Latin America', in H. Berstein (ed.), *Underdevelopment and Development*, Middlesex : Penguin, 1978, 76.

42 Z. Davidian, *Economic Disparity Among Nations : A Threat to Survival in a Globalized World*, Calcutta : Oxford University Press, 1994, p. xvii.

43 L. Thurow, *Head to Head: The Coming Economic battle Among japan, Europe and America*, St. Leonards: Allen and Unwin, 1992, p. 16).

44 For a discussion of this issue see R. Rothstein "Limits and Possibilities of Weak Theory: Interpreting North-South", in R. Rothstein (ed.), *The Evolution of Theory in International Relations*, Columbia: University of South California Press, 1991, p. 147.

45 I. Wallerstein, 'World –System Versus World-Systems; A Critique', in A. G. Frank and B. Gills (eds.), *The World System: Five Hundred Years or Five Thousand?*, London: Routledge, 1993, pp. 292-296.

46 T. Hopkins and I. Wallerstein, *World Systems Analysis: Theory and Methodology*, London: Sage, 1982, p. 47.

47 Ibid

48 Ibid.

49 T. Lewellen, *Dependency and Development: An Introduction to Third world*, Westport: Bergin and Garvey, 1995, p. 50.

50 B. Assuon, Thoughts on the Significance of Meiji-japan's Experience of Modern development for the Future Education in Ghana-Africa, Tokyo: IDE, 1992, p. 48.

51 J. Oweye, *Japan's Policy in Africa*, Lewiston: Edwin Mellen, 1992, p. 151.

52 F. Fukuyama, *Trust: The Social Virtues and the Creation of Prosperity*, London: Hamish

Hamilton, 1995.
53 Adam Smith *An Inquiry into the Nature and Causes of the Wealth of Nations*, edited by K. Sutherland, Oxford, New York: Oxford University Press, 1993, p. 30).
54 One analyst who is quite knowledgeable about Mazruiana has indeed used this very term, culturology, in a sense broadly similar to our usage. See Alamin Mazrui, 'The African Impact on American Higher Education: Ali Mazrui's Contribution', in P. Morewedge (ed.), *The Scholar between Thought and Experience: A Biographical Festschrift in Honor of Ali A. Mazrui*, Global Publications: Institute of Global Cultural Studies, 2001, p. 13.
55 Ali A.Mazrui, 'From Social Darwinism to Current Theories of Modernization: A Tradition of Analysis', *World Politics*, vol. 21, 1968, pp. 69.
56 Fukuyama, *Trust,* p. 14.
57 See Kwame Nkrumah, *The Autobiography of Kwame Nkrumah*, Edinburgh: Thomas Nelson and Sons Ltd., 1957, p. 164.
58 Examples include J. Kotkin, *Tribes: How Race, Religion and Identity Determines Success in the New Global Economy*, New York: Random House, 1992); Fukuyama, *Trust,* 1995; and L. Harrison and S. Huntington (eds.), *Culture Matters: How Values Shape Human Progress*, New York: basic Books, 2000.
59 Ibid.
60 Ibid., p. 7.
61 Ibid., p. 91.
62 I. Wallerstein, *Unthinking Social Science: The Limits of Nineteenth Century Paradigm*s, Cambridge: Polity, 1991, p. 91.
63 Mazrui, "The African Renaissance", p. 9.
64 Mazrui, "The Baganda and the Japanese", pp. 167-186.
65 Ibid., p. 167.
66 Ibid.
67 Ibid., p. 185.
68 Ibid.
69 Ali A. Mazrui, *The Social Dimension of Culture and Contemporary Expressions*, Lecture delivered at a Workshop on Culture in Sustainable Development. Investing in Cultural and Natural Endowement. Sponsored by the World Bank and UNESCO, September 28-29, 1998, p. 3.
70 For a useful discussion on this in relation to Japan in Japanese culture see Takeo, *Japan and WesterCivilizations,* p. 80.
71 Ibid., p. 173.
72 Mazrui, *The Social Dimension of Culture and Contemporary Expressions*, 1998, p. 3.

6. Between Social Theory and Public Policy: Mazruiana in Application[1]

Introduction

This chapter shares with Mazruiana three features. Firstly, it is concerned with a contemporary first-order issue in world politics. Secondly, the chapter attempts to weave different themes together and examine the connections among them. Thirdly, it uses the critical approach to scrutinize some of the predominant discourses of our time. But, for all the conceptual and methodological similarity shared with Mazruiana, it should be noted, the arguments and conclusions in the chapter are solely of this author.

I start from the premise that, if it manages to conquer the minds of policy-makers, a social theory, even one that is fundamentally self-contradictory and flawed, could prove to be truer than the most sophisticated and coherent one. This type of theory could have greater impact not only in spite of its incongruity with history and logic, but in some ways almost because of that contradiction. On the basis of this premise, I shall attempt to demonstrate that 1) the idea of the clash of civilizations, which is an aspirant for discursive hegemony, has serious empirical and logical defects; 2) the specter of such a clash is nevertheless haunting the world; and 3) under the circumstances, it is imperative not to succumb to the idea which is, in effect, an ideological Frankenstein inimical to global peace and harmony. The September 2001 terrorist attacks in the United States will provide the context for the discussion.

It must be noted from the outset that it is difficult to interrogate the dominant discourse in the aftermath of the terrorist attacks without seeming to condone terrorism. This is partly so because emotions are still raw. True, the attacks on the Twin Towers and on the Pentagon represent abominable cruelty. But does everything that has been officially said and done in response have to pass unchallenged? Should scholarly judgment be perverted by excessive concern with political correctness?

In any case I propose to analyze this subject in relation to the complex relationship between social theory and public policy and corroborate how ideas influence behavior by looking into the role played by policy-makers in this context.

What I call secular theocracy and postmodern terrorism are used in the paper as the central concepts for unraveling the connection between social theory and public policy. Secular theocracy represents a system of ideas that mixes science and religion and religion and politics with the intent of establishing a regime of truth. The latter usage is also consistent with the Mazruiana definition of theocracy as "a political system that uses God as a point of reference for policy making and makes God the focus of political morality."[2] Samuel Huntington's "the clash of civilizations" thesis, as well as the rhetoric of some of the current US leaders, can be regarded as secularized theocracy in this sense. Postmodern terrorism, on the other hand, shelters in tradition and exploits the fruits of modernity to achieve its goals, whatever these goals might be. Bin Laden, who is an embodiment of terrorism in the postmodern age, is said to combine the skill to utilize both the fruits of modernity such as computers and modern communications equipments while at the same time exalting traditional Islamic heritage.[3] Let it be noted also that the choice of the concepts of "secular theocracy" and "post-modern terrorism" is made only out of consideration of their descriptive rather than evaluative values. As loosely used in this chapter, a social theory is simply a more or less coherent, often normatively-driven idea aimed at intermediating, explaining, and predicting large scale events in human affairs. On the other hand, a public policy is the aggregate of the actions of the "legitimate" decision makers, taken in the name of a collectivity of individuals or groups.

Advanced by one of the most famous authors of our time, seemingly embraced by some of the political and military decision-makers of the most powerful nation in the world and orchestrated by the powerful, agenda-setting media of communications, the specter of the clash of civilizations is haunting the world at the dawn of the new century. There may be periods of détente between civilizations as there were moments of relaxation of tension between the superpowers during the Cold War period. But the clash of civilizations is here to stay. What I am suggesting here is neither the ingenuity of Huntington's idea nor the need for its glorification, but rather the opposite.

We now know, for better or worse, that the post-Cold War system, or the new world order as some would perhaps prefer to call it, came into effect not with the collapse of the Berlin Wall in November 1989. Instead, the new system greeted us with the collapse of the Twin Towers in New York on the 11th of September, 2001. This is not to say that just 19 individuals, however determined, changed the international system on their own. True, the actions of these individuals were consequential, however evil. But the terrorist attack was not the sole agent of the transformation. The more fundamental cause was perhaps the discursive practices in the form of secular theocracy that had been produced and reproduced over time, both before and after the terrorist attacks. In other words, the attack provided the *precipitating* cause for what appears to be a paradigm shift. The other prerequisites for such a shift were already more or less in place. In the words of Michael MccGwire, the other prerequisites for a paradigm shift are: a) an *impulse* for change, deriving from *shared fears* and a *common vision*; b) the absence or removal of *obstacles* to change, and; c) an *engine* of change.[4]

That said, here is the path that this chapter follows to accomplish its tasks. First, it elaborates how the seeds of secularized theocracy were able to germinate and nurture in the intellectual and political climate of the brief post-Cold War period and how they eventually laid the basis for the interaction of social theory and public policy, and how the interaction ultimately transformed world politics. Then it examines the effect of postmodern terrorism on secularized theocracy in the specific context of the attacks in New York and Washington.

Although the clash of civilizations is upon us, it does not represent a system; it is merely a manifestation of an enduring feature of the new system. The type of system, which eventually emerges out of the interplay between secular theocracy and postmodern terrorism, would be something like a Postmodern Theocracy. This is so because as the conflict between postmodern terrorism and secularized theocracy intensifies, terrorism becomes the tactic of choice of secularized theocrats as much as of postmodern terrorists and therefore "terrorism," having become the tactics of both sides, would become a redundant term, and lose its descriptive value. Given that terrorism is a behavioral pattern rather than a cultural attribute, there are certain actions of states, ands not just of groups such as al Qaeda, which would come to qualify as terrorist.

One recent example relates to the American treatment, or rather mistreatment, of the captives of the war in Afghanistan. The US leaders continued to refer to these individuals as detainees or illegal combatants and not prisoners of war. The aim was to deprive the captives of their rights to be treated humanely in line with the Geneva Convention of 1949. But by any definition, not least by the US's own characterization of the conflict in which the individuals were captured, the captives were prisoners of war, however asymmetric the kind of warfare they were engaged in.

America's reluctance to implement what was stipulated in the Geneva Convention regarding the need for humane treatment of prisoners of war was based on one simple, but flawed, logic: since the terrorists do not care about international law when they massacre civilians, demolish landmark buildings, blow up airplanes etc., America should similarly not bind itself with international law in dealing with these individuals. Although not officially admitted as such, the US decision makers know that their approach was wrong. But the apparent justification was that so are the operational norms of terrorists. Indeed, it is true that terrorists do not show any concern for laws, domestic or international. But this fact cannot be used as a valid premise for concluding that therefore the US should also behave in the same way. Put simply, two wrongs do not make right. Although at least one top British politician has expressed concern, in reference to the apparent US mistreatment of former Taliban and al Qaeda members, that "We are not going to allow terrorists to reduce us to the level of barbarians."[5] This, however, this seems exactly the destination towards which the world is fast drifting. Hence, the reason why one can in time dispense with "terrorism" in the "postmodern terrorism."

Likewise, as the confrontation between postmodern terrorism and secularized theocracy gets entrenched, the secular façade of the "secularized theocracy" can give way to theocracy, rendering the modifier *secular* both useless and misleading. In the end, what we could have is a system characterized by the struggle among different postmodern theocracies.

A Paradigm Shift?

In theory as well as in practice the September terrorist attacks have transformed our understanding of world politics at least in two major ways. On the one hand, it was the last nail in the coffin of the post Cold War triumphant idea of "the end of history." On the other hand, the incident has brought to life the self-fulfilling prophesy of the clash of civilizations. I attempt below to tackle the issues associated with these generalizations beginning with a brief review of what happened on that fateful day in September, and why.

Terrorism is, to use a Mazruiana definition, a "deliberate creation of specialized terror among civilians, through the use of violence, in order to promote political ends."[6] The purpose-oriented nature of what happened in the second week of September 2001 is betrayed by the careful coordination and planning that apparently went into the destructive project. The specialized and violent nature of the act also needs no description here for the media of communications has done that so graphically.

Although the perpetrators of the callous act have not lived to confess the specific ends of their acts, there is in general a shared view that it was politically motivated. But caution is required in describing the goals of terrorist acts. As Mazrui put it:

> Here we must distinguish between ultimate goals and immediate targets. The ultimate goals include an ambition to gain a hearing for causes, which would otherwise go unheard, and to make a contribution towards the realization of those causes. The immediate target is the manipulation of fear as a mechanism of combat in the context of wide publicity.[7]

Then, what was *the ultimate goal* of the September 11th terrorists? Was it to attract international attention to the plight of the Pales-

Paradigm Lost, Paradigm Regained

tinians? Was it intended to make the point to the world that the US is not an invincible superpower? Or was it to force a policy change? Of course, the three goals are not necessarily mutually exclusive. Having no clues as to the specific goal of the terrorists, we can only speculate. But whatever the goal, abhorrence for the US and its policies, or at least a disdain for them, is believed to be at the center of the picture. What is clearer is *the immediate target* of the terrorists. The Twin Towers of the World Trade Center, the Pentagon, and perhaps another landmark of symbolic significance in the US were the intended immediate targets. The decision to hit these targets was no doubt influenced by the *wide publicity* the terrorists sought to attract, and which they received. It can be said that the terrorists also achieved another purpose of theirs, which was "to manipulate fear as a mechanism of combat."[8]

The horrific destruction caused by the attacks was in many ways beyond the bounds of imagination. In terms of the immediate causalities, the acts were tragic beyond description. Therefore, the collective indignation of the world at large, which followed the attacks, stands to reason. What was perhaps less reasonable, especially from the point of view of the long-term international stability, was the ideological, religious and civilizational colors with which global terrorism was thereafter painted.

It is remarkable that while people in the US were understandably outraged by the terrorist strikes, there had not emerged a widely shared understanding of how the threat from global terrorism was to be perceived. According to a TIME opinion poll taken shortly after the attacks, 62 per cent Americans supported that the US should declare war as a result of the attack. At the same time, 61 percent of the respondents said they were not sure whom Congress should declare war against.[9]

Against the background of such a vacuum the relentless search began in earnest to put an ideological face on the enemy. *The End of History* and *The Clash of Civilizations* were two of the major "metatheories" competing for the minds of scholars and policy makers in the years following the end of the Cold War. However, each had to wait until that fateful date in September before one was to be crowned as the ultimate metatheory. Following the attacks, many people of power and influence began to view the war against terrorism as heralding the "clash of civilizations."

Those who did not share the idea of the clash of civilizations also held onto their own "theories." First, there are those for whom "the new war" heralded the beginning of the Third World War. This group resorted to drawing analogies between what happened on September 11th and the Japanese attack on Pearl Harbor.[10] Others viewed "the new war," if not the *casus belli* itself, in more sympathetic terms, as a precursor to "the new imperialism."[11]

As the new war is very much like the Cold War, still others suggested adding that therefore "the New Cold War" or the second cold war best captured what the new war is all about.[12] Still another group saw the conflict as representing a clash not between the West and Islam as such, but a clash between the latter and modernity.[13] On closer inspection, this last brand of argument appears to be merely a simplified version of the idea of the clash of civilizations expressed in more generic terms. The reasoning involved here is that since the West has long overcome the forces that stood in the way of modernity, it is unquestionably modern, or even postmodern according to some. The West also represents "a civilization." And so does Islam. It therefore follows that the clash between Islam and modernity is at the same time a clash between civilizations.

Kofi Annan, the Secretary General of the United Nations, speaking at the opening session the 56th General Assembly, also shared his vision of the future with member states. He said that the world was now faced with two choices—the choice of the path of the so called the clash of civilizations which is based on the exaggeration of differences among us, and the path of peace and progress. The General Secretary's vision of the future thus entailed three major components: 1) that the future is dangerously uncertain; 2) that, though premised on exaggerated differences, the continued perception of humanity in terms of civilizational categories could lead to disastrous consequences; and 3) that it is not impossible to avert the clash of civilizations given the political will of those who shape public opinion and make decisions.

It may be useful here to note that President George Bush's speech to the same General Assembly was devoid of the clarity of Kofi Annan's remarks. The gist of Bush's speech is summed up in his own words: "if you are not with us, you are against us." In this "good versus evil" speech, it was as if Bush was saying that the US had made its mind; it would choose the path of the clash of civilizations because America knows that its civilization would triumph, because it represents a superior form of civilization. Just like the terrorists hijacked the planes and crashed them into the Twin Towers, be realized that a civilization can be hijacked and pitted against "other" civilizations. The point here is not that the war on terrorism was unjustified. But instead, it is about a hijacking of an entire "civilization" in the name of defending it; it is about elevating what could have only been seen as a case of emergency and responded to accordingly; it is, in other words, about excessively ideologizing the conflict. I will further substantiate this point later in the chapter.

As indicated above, owing in part to their relative coherence and elaborate details, it was for "the end of history" and "the clash of civilizations" theses that the events on September 11th and what followed thereafter carried an enormous implication. How these grand hypotheses changed the world and have themselves changed as a result of the events is discussed below.

The End of the End of History

In 1989, in the heat of the euphoria generated by the implosion of what was then the Soviet Union, Francis Fukuyama advanced a historical hypothesis reminding us that the end of history had finally arrived. By the end of history, or endism, what Fukuyama meant was primarily that history as known in the West, as the struggle between liberal democracy on the one hand and "other" ideologies on the other, had come to an end subsequent to the "final" victory of the former. A related thesis of Fukuyama was that with the end of history, what was awaiting the world was an era of prosperity and peace, if not in the conflict-ridden and undemocratic states of the periphery, at least in the core countries.

For the most part, events on the ground did not entirely falsify endism, until the 11th day of September. But a hypothesis that has not been falsified does not necessarily mean that, even in the absence of a verification, that would make it an *ipso facto* valid one. It was the September terrorist attacks that brought home the point that history had not ended, at any rate not forever, as Fukuyama claimed. Articles in journals and newspapers quickly captured this, as borne out by their titles such as: *The End of Our Holiday from History*,[14] *The End of the End of History*.[15] One of the very first serious essays dealing with the attacks also pointed out: "The 1990s were a lucky decade, a fool's paradise. But we had not arrived at the end of history, not by a long shot."[16]

Endism (as well as the clash of civilizations thesis) has in fact major logical, philosophical, and empirical contradictions that could not have made it a sound basis for predicting what lies ahead.[17] But, as indicated above, it was what happened on September 11th and what followed thereafter which ascertained in clearer terms the deficiency of endism. The incident underscored that what lies ahead was at best a time of uncertainty. Fukuyama had certainly not foreseen the fragility of an interdependent world and how an action by a determined group of individuals, however small the group, could wreak havoc in the global village. The fundamental question therefore becomes, where and why did Fukuyama get it wrong?

First, Fukuyama's theory wrongly assumed that liberal democracy is an island onto itself. As he put it in his famous book, *The End of History and the Last Man:* "[i]n many respects, the historical and post-historical will maintain parallel but separate existences, with relatively little interaction between them."[18] Fukuyama thus wrongly assumed that the conflict in the periphery is unrelated to the core, or would be viewed as such by those at the receiving end. In other words, he failed to see the vulnerability of "the post-historical" to the consequences of the resentment from "the historical." Fukuyama missed the iron logic of the imperative of interdependence and interpenetration of core and periphery. Samuel Huntington's idea of the clash of civilizations similarly disregarded the legacy of interactions between different "civilizations." I shall return to the analysis of Huntington's position in a short while. Thus, it can be argued that the reification of endism gave rise to a false consciousness of a perpetual peace and led public policy officials to adopt an attitude of indifference towards issues of concern to the periphery, and that the resultant perception of the "other" in these terms pushed the grievance to a boiling point.

Second, endism got it wrong in viewing states both in the "historical" and "post-historical" worlds as the primary actors in global politics.[19] Even though attempts have been made to link the perpetrators of the September attacks to the states that "sponsor or harbor" them[20] or to states that have "failed,"[21] the primary driving forces behind the attacks were groups who neither claim nor aspire for statehood. Fukuyama disregarded, or failed to notice what James N. Rosenau has called "the skill revolution" as a result of which people are now capable of assessing competently "where they fit in international affairs and how their behavior can be aggregated into significant collective outcomes."[22] Disregarding in this way the power of individuals and small groups in influencing the course of history was therefore another Achilles Heel of endism.

Fukuyama has in any case come forward after the terrorist attacks to tell why the rival "theory" of endism, namely Samuel Huntington's "clash of civilizations," is flawed and, at least by implication, why he still thinks endism is not a sore loser following the attacks. In Fukuyama's own words: "[t]he current conflict is not part of a clash of civilizations in the sense that we are dealing with cultural zones of equal standing; rather, it is symptomatic of a rear-guard action by those who are threatened by modernization, and thus by its moral component, respect for human rights."[23] In the same piece, Fukuyama went on to liken the conflict between "theocracy and secularism" in contemporary Muslim world to the struggle in the 16th and 17th century Christian Europe "when sectarian struggles between Christian sects throughout Europe exposed the impossibility of a religious consensus on which to base a political rule."[24]

What can one make of Fukuyama's aspiration to make endism compatible in these terms with the prevailing situation? First, it is open to question if the current conflict indeed arose out of the struggle between the forces of modernity and Islam in the above sense. The second, and perhaps most important, point to note is the conflict has without a doubt put an end to the short life of "the end of history" thesis. In Fukuyama's own new formulation mentioned above, the clock of history has now been turned back at least 400 years. Again, if the current conflict is one of Islam's clash with modernity, and given the fact that the "West" is the undisputed torchbearer of this modernity, then it becomes problematic to continue to hold the view of "the ultimate" victory of liberal democracy which "the end of history" thesis had so prematurely declared.

The Invention of the Clash of Civilizations

In 1993 Samuel Huntington advanced the idea of the clash of

civilizations, or clashism for short, and maintained that the fundamental source of conflict in the new world will not be primarily ideological or primarily economic; the clash of civilizations will dominate global politics.[25] As for why this should be so, Huntington reasoned: 1) there are fundamental differences between civilizations (which he classified into seven or eight); 2) as a result of globalization there will be more interaction between them and this would in turn lead to increased civilizational consciousness; and 3) therefore, civilizations would clash.

First it must be pointed out that, given the historical inter-penetration of civilizations, it is hard to defend the core presupposition of clashism: the distinctiveness of civilizations. In order to challenge clashism effectively in its most coherent form and attempt to undermine its underlying ideology, I shall however assume in the discussion below that there are such distinct civilizations.

In disagreement with Huntington, it can be argued, also, that there is no unambiguous historical evidence to suggest that increased consciousness about one's "civilizational" identity would in itself lead to a clash of civilizations. Both logic and history lend support instead to the contrasting view that increased interaction among civilizations, which precedes increased consciousness, engenders mutual respect rather than confrontation between them since such interaction always generates a cumulative experience in conflict resolution. "De-Westernization and indigenization of the elite is occurring in many non-Western countries at the same time that Western, usually American cultures, styles, and habits become more popular among the masses," emphasized Huntington.[26] But it is unclear here, too, how such observation supports the inevitability of the clash of civilizations. Cultures, styles, and habits constitute the core elements of any civilization. Therefore, it follows that increased interaction between civilizations should instead lead to co-operation rather than collision.

To substantiate his idea and make it more scientific, Huntington refers to the proportions by which the intra-regional trade rose between 1980 and 1989.[27] It is worth noting, however, that the time frame of the data is altogether irrelevant; the data is, in fact, so irrelevant as to render it misleading. If Huntington's intention were to show, as he put it, how "the Velvet curtain of culture has replaced the iron curtain of ideology," why would he have to use data for the period *between* 1980 and 1989? The iron curtain began to be torn down *in* 1989, not *before* 1989.

The idea of "kin-country syndrome," which Huntington sought to substantiate taking the case of the Gulf war,[28] is similarly flawed. Had civilizational fault lines been the major lines along which the post-Cold war battles were to be fought, as Huntington's hypothesis postulated, it would have been inconceivable for a Sunni Muslim Iraq to invade a fellow Sunni Muslim Kuwait in the first place.

Samuel Huntington also went on to declare: "[a] Confucian-Islamic military connection has come into being…and the flow of weapons and weapons technology is generally from East Asia to the Middle East."[29] If there were evidence that the Confucian-Islamic connection has indeed come into being, as Huntington claimed, it would undermine his kin-country argument mentioned above. It should be noted, however, that in terms of the value of weapons, the West by far surpasses East Asia as a major source of arms to the Middle East.[30] In either case, again, one of the central propositions of Huntington's social theory would be seriously undermined.

Despite the flaws such as the above, clashism appears to be influential in some circles. Before I examine what this means for international affairs, it is the sources and manifestations of the power of clashism that I must now address. A good deal of attention has been focused on clashism since the September terrorist attacks in the United States. The prevailing views regarding the relationship between the current conflict and the clash of civilizations can be divided into three broad and inevitably overlapping categories.

Paradigm Lost, Paradigm Regained

First, there are those who insist that the current conflict has already paved the way for the clash of civilizations and that, regardless of what we do or do not do, the trend is irreversible, although it is still possible to mitigate the negative consequences of such a clash through a pursuit of well-thought policies. Second, there are those who see a heightened awareness of the clash of civilizations as a result of the current conflict. For this very same reason, according to this school, the clash would and could be reversed or contained. The third school insists that whether or not the conflict would move in the direction of a clash of civilizations would largely depend on our choice of the course of action. It must be added that even those who see the "theory" of the clash of civilizations as fundamentally flawed allow for the possibility of its fulfillment.

The above views are anchored in one of the two basic assumptions abouts *reflexive predictions,* or prophecies that are prone to be self-fulfilling or self-frustrating.[31] If people are sufficiently convinced about the likelihood of an impending danger, their very awareness - and the corresponding changes in behavioral patterns - could avert the danger. There are therefore those observers of contemporary world politics who pin their hopes on the theoretical possibility that the chances for the clash of civilizations to become a reality are about the same as the chances for its aversion.

The question which inevitably follows from this is, how do we know that the era of the clash of civilizations has not already set in, and if it has not set in yet, how do we tell when such a time eventually arrives, assuming that it would? Contemporary debate on the clash of civilizations raises such basic questions. But as yet there have been few clear-cut answers from the proponents of the clash of civilizations or its critiques.

Perhaps one of the reasons for the overlap in the above categories as well as the persistent questions that are associated with them is the underlying disagreement on the essence of a clash of civilizations and its forms or manifestations. There is seldom a limit, at any rate an explicit one, to the meaning of the clash of civilizations. Clarifying definitional issues would therefore constitute a necessary step for expounding the contending meanings or interpretations of the phenomena.

One such step would be to make a clear distinction and consistently stick to the usage of a chronological definition of a clash of civilizations: a clash of civilizations as something that had started or taken place much earlier; a clash of civilizations as a post-Cold War phenomena; a clash of civilizations as a long process that commenced on September 11th; or a clash of civilizations as something that has not happened yet, but is either inevitable in the years ahead or, alternatively, avoidable if the requisite measures are taken. A useful suggestion here may be to adapt Mazruiana's classification of the clash of civilizations into different stages and types based on its nature and intensity as enslaving, genocidal, imperial, and hegemonic.[32]

To begin with a clear statement of position in regard to the above definitional issues, I hypothesized in the opening pages of this chapter that the clash of civilizations is upon us. I shall try below to clarify further my understanding of the clash of civilizations against the backdrop of rival interpretations and then proceed to elaborate how the dynamics of the clash of civilizations are unfolding.

As outlined above, the clash of civilizations thesis, or clashism, exhibited from its very inception, flaws generally akin to endism despite the structural orientation of the former and historical orientation the latter. But, ironically, while ending the short life of the end of history, the September terrorist attacks put a new lease of life on the clash of civilizations. One indication of the popularity of "the clash of civilizations" thesis is the predominance of the clashist concepts and views reflected in academic discourse and policy statements. Even those who grasped the broader implications of the trend and genuinely insisted that the clash of civilizations was undesirable seemed to be using the same framework as a point of reference and think in terms imposed on them by its ideology. Another related indication of the growing interest in the idea of the clash of civilizations even among ordinary people was the big upsurge in the aftermath of the attack in sales of Huntington's book, *The Clash of Civilizations and the Remaking of the World Order.*[33]

It is one of the ironies of current affairs that the same terror attack could end "the end of history" while at the same time reinvigorate "the clash of civilizations" thesis. A significant number of people both in the media of communications and policy-makers in the United States have shown the tendency of swearing allegiance to the clash of civilizations idea more than to endism.

Three basic reasons underlay the attractions of clashism. One is its distorting simplicity: "us" versus "them." Philosophically, clashism is less sophisticated than the other contending "theories." Therefore, to some it was more palatable. It was a handy desideratum, however simplistic, for the interpretation of the present, and prediction of what was to come as well as for what was to be done under the circumstances.

Apart from its simplicity, another source of the attractions of Huntington's thesis to those attracted towards it is that the idea represented not only a clash between "us" and "them"; it is also one between a "superior" and an "inferior" civilization. Framed in this way, such a stereotype makes clashism a more acceptable theory for "it is a guarantee of our self-interest; it is a projection upon the world of our own value, our own position, and our own rights... [It] is the fortress of our own tradition and behind its defense we can continue to feel ourselves safe in the position we occupy."[34]

A third appealing quality of clashism, which is again embedded in its simplicity, is the presumed absence of overlap or affinity among "civilizations." Each civilization is unique.[35] This feature of the clash of civilization argument introduces an element of rigidity unlike endism which allows, at least in theory, for the possibility of the expansion of the borders of "the self" to include "the other" since, in the words of the author of endism, "the boundary line between the post–historical and historical worlds is changing rapidly and is therefore hard to draw."[36]

It should also be noted that the clash of civilizations text shares with the Marxian discourse a contradictory logic in its insistence that one form of social (dis)order is imminent while at the same time urging that something must be done to affect, though not necessarily prevent, it. The basic difference between the manifestos of Marx and Huntington lies in the utopian vision of the former as opposed to the pessimism of the latter. But just like Marxism, clashism also seems to have almost changed, or at least seems to be changing the course of history. Historians have asked in the past in regard to Marxism how such illogical "theory" came to have so powerful and enduring influence. It seems almost likely that future historians would likewise raise similar questions in regard to the idea of the clash of civilizations.

However that may be, Samuel Huntington has given us a desideratum of destruction, unconcerned, it seems, about the long-term consequences of his "theory." Perhaps it is considerations such as this which led one observer to comment, in reference to Huntington, that: "[i]t may come as a striking revelation that the West also has its hordes of fundamentalists, of the armchair kind—but although they don't resort to jet-turned-to-missile suicide squads—they are just as deadly."[37]

Another observer, William Pfaff, also remarked:

> This idea [of the clash of civilizations] is identical to that which a century ago saw race war as the world's future. That forecast convinced Hitler. We do not want to see that repeated. War between civilizations is a pernicious idea and only an idea, not a reality. It must be resisted.[38]

The significance of Pfaff's observation can be seen from two sides. On the one side, the passage is a reference to the flawed premise and similarly flawed generalization constituting the idea of the clash of civilizations. Viewed from another side, the statements essentially represent an appeal to the effect that the attractions of the model of the clash of civilizations be resisted. What is even more significant in the above observation is the conclusion that can be drawn from it, that even an idea that is devoid of cogency and broader normative appeal could turn itself into a self-fulfilling prophecy. The consequences of our acts spring from the acts themselves whether the basis on which the acts are made are themselves flawed or not. It does not make much sense, therefore, to argue that if the idea of the clash of civilizations is based on a faulty premise, why bother to appeal for resistance against it.

In the above passage, Pfaff does not of course say that the clash of civilizations is inevitable. And yet his observation does suggest that, unless strongly resisted, the prophecy about the clash of civilizations could fulfill itself. Even a pernicious social theory, if it elicits in the realm of public policy-making a significant level of inter-subjective understanding, a shared knowledge as well as expectation, its realization will not be beyond the bounds of possibility.

The Discourse of Clashism

In a 1997 prophetic and forward-looking critique of Huntington's new book about "the clash of civilizations," F. S. Tipson wrote the following:

> His [Huntington's] book conveys a challenge,
> like he wants us to refute him,
> Daring us, by scaring us, to doubt him or dispute him.
> Which is fine for academic-argument-displaying,
> As long as someone powerful won't act on what he's saying...

> Politicians prone to pick what's overripe or rotten,
> May resurrect a culture that is gone but not forgotten,
> Building on the current state of cultural confusion,
> To craft a cult of closure or a culture of exclusion.[39]

In the wake of the September attacks, policy makers in the US, more than their counter-parts in other parts of the world, seemed to be in haste to fulfill the scenarios of clashism. There was a tendency to depict the terrorist attack as the declaration of war by Islam on Western civilization. Consequently, the military attack on Afghanistan that began on 8 October 2001 took on all the forms of a Western crusade against Islam, in spite of official assurances given to the contrary.[40] The policy-makers were justified in advocating a strong action against the perpetrators of the attacks, but putting an ideological face on an apparently invisible enemy was wrong, especially if one considers the wider implication of this for global harmony and, needless to say, the implications for the long-term interest of the United States itself.

Excerpts from the official statements of the US government support the claim about the eagerness to frame the situation in terms of clash of civilizations, whether conscious or unconscious of the long-term consequences of this form of discourse.

> The hour is coming when America will act...This is not, however, just America's fight. And what is at stake is not just America's freedom. This is the world's fight. *This is civilization's fight.* This is the fight of all who believe in progress and pluralism, tolerance and freedom.[41] (Italics added).

The above passage is taken from President George W. Bush's speech to a joint session of the US Congress on the 20th of September, 2001. It is true that in the same speech the President praised the "outpouring of support" from other friendly, including Arab and Islamic, states. But such rhetoric seemed to be just window dressing, a message of misrepresentation based on the conviction that there is no need even for the good opinion of the "other."

Those who were free from the minimal constraints of diplomatic niceties were more straightforward in revealing the new paradigm. The Reverend Franklin Graham, who was a speaker at Bush's inauguration was, for instance, reported to have remarked in reference to the September 11th attacks that, "We're not attacking Islam, but Islam has attacked us. The God of Islam is not the same God. He is not the son of God of the Christian or Judeo Christian faith. It is a different God, and I believe it is a very evil and wicked religion."[42]

In truth, what the US leaders sought most of all was a minimum moral and possibly other forms of support not from a genuinely global coalition, but from those "who believe in progress and pluralism, tolerance and freedom." None of the Arab and Islamic states alluded to in the above speech qualify as pluralistic and tolerant societies in the sense the President used the phrase. And yet it would seem that the President was fully aware of what he was talking about. If he was seeking a genuine global coalition he would not have failed to mention the UN in his long speech. But unfortunately the UN is considered to be a conglomerate of units from different (and presumably clashing) civilizations.

The pluralistic and tolerant societies the President alluded to were those that constitute the Western civilization depicted by clashism, virtually all of which are also members of the North Atlantic Treaty Organization. After all, Western civilization is a collective name given to liberal democracies. Later in the same speech, President Bush himself made this point clear: "Perhaps the NATO Charter reflects the best attitude of the world. An attack on one [NATO member] is an attack on all. *The civilized world is rallying to America's side.*"[43] (Italics mine)

Hours prior to the President's speech, the Taliban leaders, or more precisely the Afghan Council of Elders, which is composed of religious clerics, put out a declaration stating, among other things, that they would wage a holy war (*jihad*) if they were attacked by America. In response to the statement about the prospect of *jihad* by the Taliban, President Bush also made it clear that: "[f]reedom and fear, justice and cruelty, have always been at war, and *we know that God is not neutral between them.*"[44] Perhaps it is observations such as this one, which led Lynn Mitchell, the theology expert, to comment that "Bush, as a conservative Christian, appeared to be asserting that Satan was behind the Sept. 11 attacks. [Bush] did not leave Christianity at the door when he entered the White House."[45]

It is hard, therefore, to tell if the President's statement mentioned above represented in essence any thing less than an American declaration of *Jihad*. There is not much that sets the substance of the President's statement apart from that expressed by the Taliban, or Bin Laden for that matter, except for the fact that the former was not made by "religious clerics." "If you are not with us, you are against us," was also how President Bush imposed the binary opposition upon a range of essentially different political units. If Michael Doran's interpretation is to be relied upon, the purpose of Bin Laden's actions was also to make the point to the Arab and Islamic Worlds that: "You are either with the idol—worshipping enemies of God or you are with the true believers."[46] Perplexed by such incredible parallelism between the language used by Bin Laden's camp on the one hand and George Bush on the other, one commentator has an occasion to ask: "[d]id they [:Bin Laden and his associates] learn from us[:the West, and more specifically the Bush Administration] or did we learn from them?"[47] An American critic Lance Morrow was similarly straightforward in his observation that: "[t]he American street is now willing to employ ayatollah vocabularies—to think in fatwas."[48]

In the same speech referred to above, the President reminded the audience that the goal of the terrorist organization such as Bin Laden's Al Qaeda was "not making money, its goal is *re-making the world*."[49]

Paradigm Lost, Paradigm Regained

Upon hearing this utterance, one unpleasant association which springs to mind, almost instinctively, is the title of Samuel Huntington's book: The Clash of Civilizations and the *Re-Making of World Order*. (Italics mine) If such correspondence in phraseology were a mere coincidence, how about the President's "axis of evil" suggestive remark made in reference to Iraq, Iran, and North Korea in his State of the Union speech on January 29, 2002? Was it just a paraphrase of Huntington's "Islamic-Confucian connection," referred to above? If so, is the President also following Huntington's Machiavellian advice in regard to this alleged Islamic-Confucian connection that the US policy-makers should "exploit differences and conflicts among Confucian and Islamic states"?[50] Does such reasoning provide a context for the policy stance the US has adopted in respect to the "axis of evil?" In short, does the President subscribe to clashism? Frankly, it is difficult to answer these questions with certainty. But it is fair to say that the President is familiar with clashism and his policies are perhaps informed by it.

Shortly after the bombardment of Afghanistan began, Samuel Huntington also came forward on the pages of *The New York Times* to say with a suppressed, if barely concealed, sense of vindication and self-congratulation that "the ongoing conflict could move in [the clash of civilization] direction."[51] What is more, Huntington lauded the Bush administration for acting "exactly the right way."[52] It is therefore well within the reach of logic to suspect that clashism is indeed influencing the opinion of those individuals whose decisions are consequential for global harmony.

In the interview he gave to *The New York Times*, Huntington admitted that the Confucian-Islamic alliance may not turn out to be true (as initially postulated by his "theory")—instead, he maintained, "the conflict could be between Islam and the West."[53] This counter-historical attempt of rearranging events to fit an explanatory pattern was presumably necessitated by the fact that India and China stood on the side of the United States, rather than with "Islam" in the current conflict. By trying to salvage his "theory" in light of the new developments, however, Huntington did not perhaps realize that he was further depriving his "social theory" of the little logical coherence it originally possessed.

The apparent reluctance of the US policy makers to view the situation in ways other than clash of civilizations is also evident, as indicated earlier, from the virtually complete disregard of the UN, despite the increasingly loud voices that had been calling for the latter's involvement in response to the challenges of global terrorism.

And yet some observers have argued that what happened on September 11th would usher in an era of US multilateralism. But this did not happen. And neither does it look likely in the future. At best the multilateralistic rhetoric that appeared now and then in the wake of the conflict merely represented a commitment to a tactical solidarity rather than a reflection of a long-term devotion to multilateralism.[54]

Perhaps for the same reason, within the West itself European policy-makers were more cautious than those in the US and were reluctant to succumb to the pressure to see "America's new war" in clashist terms. One notable exception is the Italian Prime Minster Silvio Berlusconi who was apparently eager to go down in history as more Catholic than the Pope himself. In a statement that reads like a quote from Huntington's book, Berlusconi made a sweeping judgment that was unbecoming of a statesman of his stature. He said: "Western Civilization is superior to Islamic civilization."[55]

Other European leaders were not openly as belligerent. Speaking to German Parliament, Chancellor Schroeder said one week after the terror attacks that: "…last week's devastating attacks on landmark US building was not a 'clash of civilizations.'"[56] British Prime Minster Tony Blair also expressed his confidence that the coalition that was to be formed to wage war on global terrorism would include "Arab and Islamic countries."[57] France expressed its support in similar terms.[58] The Minister of Foreign Affairs of France, Hubert Vedrine, has even cautioned: "..it was important to avoid a 'clash of civilizations' between the West and Islam in the wake of the [September 11] attacks."[59] Dominique Moisi of the French Institute for International Relations also said: "[t]he sort of crusade that would create a 'clash of civilizations' war makes Europe really nervous. We cannot afford that."[60]

It should be added, however, that although Europe in general appeared unwilling to readily embrace the idea of the clash of civilizations, it seemed to have reluctantly accepted the war on terrorism in terms generally defined by President George Bush thereby implicitly appropriating the binary distinction forced upon them by the dominant discourse.

Chancellor Schroeder of Germany reiterated in the aforementioned speech that: "this is not a clash of civilizations. This is a struggle for civilization…"[61] What did the Chancellor exactly mean when he said, "this is a struggle for civilization?" One point worth noting is that Schroeder's reference is to a civilization in the singular. Is the reference here to the "Western" civilization or is it to a "world" civilization? Though the second interpretation is also not logically out of reach, it would seem that it is the first interpretation that underlies Schroeder's statement. He seemed indeed to be talking about the struggle for "our" civilization, the "Western" civilization. If this is so, then the statement is perfectly compatible with clashism, that is, if one struggles for "one's" civilization the struggle is willy-nilly against the "other" civilization(s). It is obvious to all that neither Osama Bin Laden nor his al Qaeda is a civilization whereas Islam is, and it is also Islam that Bin Laden has identified himself with.

In the Arab/Islamic world as well as in the other regions, there was a heightened awareness of the danger of viewing the events of September 11th and the subsequent US response as a clash of civilizations. According to the Iranian News Agency, President Khatami of Iran said: "Unfortunately, the recent inhuman acts in the United States have become an excuse for those who see their interests in clashes with

Muslim civilization to provoke anger against Muslims..."[62]

During her visit to the US in the first week after the terror attacks, the President of Indonesia refrained from characterizing the situation that emerged following September 11th in clash of civilizations terms. An editorial on *The Japan Times* also warned: "If America and its allies brand more nations as 'hostile,' the war would expand, possibly leading to a confrontation similar to the 'clash of civilizations' predicted by US historian Samuel P. Huntington."[63]

Although the Muslim/Arab leaders have generally eschewed the concept of civilizations in the context of the conflict, the pressure from the trendy term was so outstanding to force some of them to its usage. During a joint Press Conference with Prime Minister Tony Blair in London, King Abdullah of Jordan said that Jordan "as a civilized nation" would support the fight against terrorism.[64] At the same time, on the other side of the Atlantic, President Bush was proclaiming, "the attack was directed against civilization itself." Although the term "civilization" conventionally denotes a superior form of culture, its connotation is different and can even be contradictory depending upon the culture and the historical movement to which one subscribes. The perspective from which the term was used by President Bush and King Abdullah appears to be contradictory in this sense. President Bush's usage rules out the possibility for the Hashemite Kingdom of Jordan to be part of the Western civilization, in contrast to what King Abdullah seemed to be alluding to. Abdullah's usage could be incorporated only if a civilization is defined not in spatial terms but in temporal terms, to borrow a useful phrase from Mazrui, as the age of the informal collective empire of the West.[65]

For President Bush, however, the reference was to the Western civilization, a choice perhaps made considering that the "Western" civilization is the only civilization worthy of the name. This was perhaps also a choice made out of the recognition that Huntington's classification of civilizations into five or six was far too complex and cumbersome for the President in comparison to the old, and by far the simpler, dichotomy of the civilized versus the uncivilized, the West and the rest. Such a binary distinction is an indispensable tool for the preservation of old stereotypes as much as for the formation of new ones.

From Democratic Peace to Theocratic Peace?

The issues of war and peace are widely discussed in what is known in International Relations as democratic peace theory. With the end of the Cold War, this theme received greater attention against the widespread belief that, with ideological rivalry between the East and the West having come to an end, the burning issue has become the quest for peaceful coexistence among the different states within the West itself. There have been suggestions that the expanding horizon of democracy in the world also makes the investigation of the relationship between democracy and peace all the more important.

The ideas of the 18th century German philosopher, Immanuel Kant, provided the philosophical basis for the democratic peace theory.[66] I do not intend here to evaluate empirical as well as logical evidence in support of or in opposition to this theory. Instead, what I aspire to do in this section is to only try to demonstrate that the very idea of democratic peace, like many other cardinal concepts and principles which guide contemporary international relations, was born out of religion and that there is a good deal of overlap between the ideas of democratic peace and what I call a theocratic peace.

Immanuel Kant's idea that democracies do not fight essentially classifies the world into two—the democratic camp that is at peace and the "undemocratic" camp that is at war with itself. Several centuries earlier than Kant, Islamic jurisprudence had similarly divided the world into to: *Dar al Islam*, the camp of peace and *Dar Al Herb*, the camp of war.[67]

A distinction can of course be made between the theocratic peace of the 4th century Islamic jurisprudence and the democratic peace formulated by Kant in the 17th century. For Kant the ultimate source of power is the individual. For the Islamic jurists, the will of Allah, as revealed to the Prophet lends validity and legitimacy to the idea of a theocratic peace.

But the affinity between religion and the secular democratic peace seems by far to overshadow their separation. On the one hand, as the Law of Nations was itself the product of European diplomatic history and statecraft, the "Law" of democratic peace came down from what used to be the "Law of Christian Nations," which subsequently became the "Law of Civilized Nations," and then became "the Law of Developed Nations."[68] In other words, "the transition from religious dualism to civilizational dualism, to the developmental dualism has been direct."[69]

On the other hand, both from the perspectives of the ancient idea of theocratic peace and from that of the modern democratic peace theory, "perpetual peace" lies in the realm of ideas and values rather than in the material attributes of different societies and, for both paradigms, the "camp of war" is not only at war within itself, but would ultimately pose a threat to "the camp of peace."

But even if the discursive overlap between the assumptions of the two paradigms of thought—the 4th century Islamic idea and the 18th century Western idea of democratic peace— were a mere coincidence, the correspondence itself is remarkable. Immanuel Kant was not of course alone in retelling, consciously or unconsciously, an idea that seems to have its roots in a non-Western system of thought. It had long been discovered, for instance, that some of the respectable ideas that came out of the pens of such great European thinkers as Comte, Spencer and Machiavelli, among others, had been articulated centuries earlier, and in many cases with more sharpness and profundity, by the 14th Century Muslim thinker, Ibn Khaldun.[70]

Two centuries after Immanuel Kant, Thomas Hobbes launched

the idea of "state of nature."⁷¹ Hobbes, like Kant, sought to figure out the ultimate route to peace. But unlike Kant, Hobbes's preoccupation was with peace among individuals, not among states. Hobbes argued that a central authority is a requisite condition for durable peace in a society. To underscore his point, Hobbes contrived a hypothetical state of nature where there was no central authority, where everyone was against everyone, and where life was short, nasty, and brutish. This is also, in effect, a Hobbesian *Dar al Islam* and *Dar al Harb*.

The division between *Dar al Islam* and *Dar al Harb* is also not unlike Fukuyama's dichotomy of the world into "the post-historical" and "the historical world."⁷² For the liberal school in international relations: "[o]verall, there is a 'Zone of Peace' comprising consolidated liberal democracies in the West (including Japan), gradually expanding to include new democracies. And there is a 'Zone of Conflict' where liberal democracy, international institutions, and cooperative interdependence remain in short supply."⁷³

And, now, where does Samuel Huntington's idea of the clash of civilizations fit into all this? Contemporary democratic peace theorists have understandably distanced themselves from the clash of civilizations thesis—some asserting that Huntington's theory is not supported by history or logic. ⁷⁴ There are nevertheless profound similarities between Huntington's thesis and the democratic peace theory.

Democratic peace proponents share with Samuel Huntington a basic assumption about the prospect of war between Western states: "[a] sense of shared identity among peoples who govern themselves democratically constitutes a form of in-group feeling, one that might foster animosity toward those who govern themselves differently."⁷⁵ Huntington has also said: "Military conflict among Western states is unlikely."⁷⁶ And yet democratic peace theory does not endorse "the clash of civilizations" thesis that there would inevitably be a clash between the West and the rest. It seems that the incompatibility is, however, not so much because of exceptional fallacy in the clash of civilizations thesis as viewed through the lens of a democratic peace theory.[77] It has perhaps more to do with what is rightly thought to be the undesirable implications of the very idea of the clash of civilizations. Upon a closer inspection, it becomes clear that the idea of civilizational solidarity or democratic peace (which the democratic peace theory defends) is not logically incompatible with conflict between civilizations (which the democratic peace theory rejects). This is therefore the sense in which it can be said that Samuel Huntington's clash of civilizations is a more assertive and militant, but less scientific, version of the democratic peace theory.

Democratic peace theory is normatively more conscious than the clash of civilizations thesis. The former is premised on two key assumptions: that "the West" rather than "the other" stands to benefit more from the stability and continuity of *Pax-Americana*, and that such ideas and institutions based on them can significantly influence collective behavior and outcome. It would seem that Huntington does also believe that the West is the superior force in the contemporary international system, although he is apparently convinced about the Western "superiority" so much so that he wishes to see a preemptive move against any 'civilizations' that would pose a potential threat to the West.

Ultimately, the clash of civilizations thesis and the democratic peace theory are therefore not as discordant as they seem at first glance. The difference between the two merely represents what may be called a negotiated contradiction. On balance, democratic peace theory is more inward-looking; the clash of civilizations theory is more preoccupied with what it perceives to be a conspiracy of the "other" civilizations and with the long-term threat that this would presumably pose for the West.

The myopic clashist perspective is in some ways a reflection of a disregard for the increasingly interdependent nature of the world as well as, to use James Rosenau's useful phrase,[78] the revolution in the skill of individuals. These developments have made the insularity of one civilization from another virtually impossible, if there was ever anything as such. What happened on the 11th of September, 2001 is a graphic illustration, however cruel, of the interplay of the skill revolution and interdependence in the global village.

I have indicated above that the idea of the clash of civilizations assumes a durable peace within the Western civilization itself, and that the Western civilization is a collective name given to the liberal democracies. Immanuel Kant's democratic peace thesis I referred to above is in essence a secular version of the theocratic peace that had been propagated earlier. There are now indications that the secular feature of the idea of peace and war in the West is itself in the process of being transformed. If the current intellectual and policy trends translate into a sustained pattern of behavior and lead to culture changes which inform much of public policy, would this not also mean that we are coming full circle: from theocratic peace to democratic peace and back to a 21st century version of theocratic peace?

Conclusion

So where are we headed? It is hard to give a definitive answer to the question of where we are headed. At this stage one can only guess. But, as indicated above, there are some factual clues already. In regard to the question of whether or not the current conflict could lead to the clash of civilizations, the response took one of three forms, as I have discussed in detail in the preceding pages. Some insisted that the current conflict has already opened the door for a clash of civilizations and that, regardless of what we do or do not do, the trend is now irreversible. Others saw a heightened awareness of the clash of civilizations as a result of the conflict. For this very same reason, the proponents of this view point out, the clash would be reversed. And then there are those who are firmly of the opinion that whether or not the conflict would move in the direction of a clash of civilizations depends on our choice of the course of action.

One conclusion that can be drawn is that if we continue to perceive the world through a clashist lens, a full-fledged clash of civilizations is in all probability what we would get. To put it in another way, debatable as the distinctiveness of civilizations and the inevitability of an eventual clash between them are, the inter-subjectively shared knowledge and expectation of it could lead to its fulfillment. This is so simply because, given a public policy informed by clashist ideas combined with sustained socialization into it, there is nothing which could prevent "us" from constructing our own distinctive civilizations and confronting that of the "others." Civilizational identities, like national and ethnic identities, could be constructed. To use a Mazruiana formulation, "when normative political theory predicts certain forms of human behavior, there is often room for self-fulfilling prophecies."[79]

It may be already too late to avert the clash of civilizations in the sense of mutual distrust and hatred based on exaggerated differences among peoples of different cultures. But at the minimum the clash could be made into one marked with a lasting détente. And this is a modest ambition. On the other hand, it is also possible, in theory, to turn the prophecy of a perpetual clash of civilizations into a self-frustrating one. In either case, what all this means is that, to adapt Alexander Wendt's fitting phrase,[80] a clash of civilizations is what we make of it

---

1 A shorter version of this chapter appears in the *Review of International Affairs*, vol. 2, no. 1, 46-63.
2 Mazrui (1974a: 107).
3 See A. B. Atwan, 'Inside Osama's Mountain Lair,' *The Guardian*, 12 November 2001. Also see Ajami (2001: 4).
4 For a discussion and application of this framework in a different context see MccGwire (2002: 1-28).
5 See 'World Shock As US Tortures Al Qaeda', *The East African Standard*, January 22, 2002.
6 Mazrui (1985b: 349).
7 Mazrui (1985b: 349).

Paradigm Lost, Paradigm Regained 131

8 Mazrui (1985b: 349-350).
9 *Time*, 24 September 2001, pp. 40-41.
10 See, for instance, Alex Fryer's article in *The Seattle Times*, September 12, 2001.
11 Naill Ferguson, 'Welcome to the New Imperialism,' *The Guradian*, 31 October 2001; also see Robert Kaplan, 'Afghanistan Could be the Straw that Breaks Central Asia's Back,' *The Japan Times*, October 19, 2001, p. 17. For a similar, but unsympathetic, view see Ikenberry (2002: 44-60).
12 McDougall (2002: 4).
13 Francis Fukuyama, 'Islam's Clash with Modernity,' *The Japan Times*, November 28, 2001, p. 21.
14 George Will, 'The End of Our Holiday from History,' *Voices*, September 11, 2001.
15 Fareed Zaakaria, 'The End of the End of History,' *Newsweek* September 24, 2001.
16 Ajami (2001: 15).
17 See Seifudein (2002: 2-15).
18 Fukuyama (1992: 277).
19 Fukuyama (1992: 276-277).
20 Jervis (2002: 40).
21 Walt (2002: 62).
22 Rosenau (1995: 194-195).
23 Francis Fukuyama, 'Islam's Clash with Modernity,' *The Japan Times*, 28 November 2001, p. 21.
24 Francis Fukuyama, 'Islam's Clash with Modernity,' *The Japan Times*, 28 November 2001, p. 21.
25 Huntington (1993: 22).
26 Huntington (1993: 27).
27 Huntington (1993: 27).
28 Huntington (1993: 35-36).
29 Huntington (1993: 47).
30 See for example *SIPRI Yearbook. Armaments, Disarmament and International Security*, New York: Oxford University Press, 1999, p. 426.
31 For elaboration of this theme see Mazrui (1969c: 172-188).
32 For elaboration of the classification see chapter six of this book.
33 See Giles Elgood, 'Terror Attacks Spark Worldwide Boom in Book Sales,' *Reuters*, October 23, 2001.
34 Buchanan and Cantril (1953: 53).
35 For elaboration see Huntington (1996: 28-46).
36 Fukuyama (1992: 277).
37 Pepe Escobar, 'The New Imperialism,' *Asia Times*, 6 November 2001.
38 William Pfaff, 'Dustbin Paradigm: Civilization Clash Not Ordained,, *The Japan Times*, October 18, 2001, p. 21.
39 Tipson (1997: 166-169).
40 For such assurances see for instance George Gedda, 'State Dept. No War on Islam,' *Associated Press*, 27 September 2001.

41 See The Address of President George Bush to a Joint Session of the US Congress, September 20, 2001.
42 See 'America's Hall of Shame,' *The Washington Post*, 22 November 2001.
43 See The Address of President George Bush to a Joint Session of the US Congress, September 20, 2001.
44 See The Address of President George Bush to a Joint Session of the US Congress, September 20, 2001.
45 Alan Elsner, 'Bush Demonizes 'Evil One,' *The Japan Times*, 30 October 2001, p. 19.
46 Doran (2002: p. 25).
47 Robert Fisk, 'Who is Copying Who in War of Words?' *Independent*, 11 October 2001.
48 Lance Morrow, 'Who's More Arrogant?' *Time*, 10 December 2001, p. 74.
49 See 'The Address of President George Bush,' September 20, 2001.
50 Huntington (1993: 49).
51 See 'A Head-On Collision of Alien Cultures?' *The New York Times*, 20 October 2001.
52 See 'A Head-On Collision of Alien Cultures?' *The New York Times*, 20 October 2001.
53 See 'A Head-On Collision of Alien Cultures?' *The New York Times*, 20 October 2001
54 For a brief but useful discussion on this, see George Monbiot, 'The Need for Dissent,' *The Guardian*, September 18, 2001. For a qualified but opposing view see William Pfaff, 'New Isolationism in the Wing,' *The Japan Times*, 21 September 2001, p. 18.
55 Susan Sevareid, 'Italian Premier Puts Down Islam,' *Associated Press*, 27 September 2001. Berlusconi did later apologize for his statement, see Alessandra Rizzo, 'Berlusconi Apologizes for Remarks,' *Associated Press*, 28 September 2001.
56 Emma Thomasson, 'European Leaders Lobby Bush After Attacks,' *Reuters*, September 19, 2001.
57 Emma Thomasson, 'European Leaders Lobby Bush After Attacks,' *Reuters*, September 19, 2001.
58 Emma Thomasson, 'European Leaders Lobby Bush After Attacks,' *Reuters*, September 19, 2001.
59 See Joell Diderich, 'Allies Supportive But Wary Over US Response,' *Reuters*, September 17, 2001.
60 Quoted in Paul Geitner, 'Europe Backs US, But Worries,' *Associated Press*, September 18, 2001.
61 'Schroeder Sees Winning Vote on Troops to Afghanistan,' *Reuters*, 9 November 2001.
62 See, 'Iran Advises US Against Attacking Afghans,' *Reuters*, September 17, 2001.
63 See 'Japan's Fight Against Terrorism,' *The Japan Times*, September 25, 2001, p. 18.
64 *BBC World*, November 7, 2001.
65 Mazrui (1996c: 218-219).
66 See Kant (1991).
67 For a slightly different reading see Mazrui (1994a: 362-372); also see Mazrui (1984: 291).
68 Paraphrased from Mazrui (1994a: 366).
69 Mazrui (1975: 15-17).
70 See Enan (1975: 152).

Paradigm Lost, Paradigm Regained

71 See Hobbes (1991).
72 Fukuyama (1992: 277).
73 Sorensen (1997: 254).
74 See for instance Russett, Oneal and Cox (2000: 583-608).
75 Russett, Oneal and Cox (2000: 583-608).
76 Huntington (1993: 39).
77 See for instance Schwartz and Skinner (2002: 159-172).
78 Rosenau (1995: 194-195).
79 Mazrui (1996a: 168).
80 Wendt (1992: 391-425).

7. Ideas in Words

Introduction

One of the manifestations of the genius of Ali Mazrui is his capacity to coin terminologies that are both concise and expressive. Although few Mazruiana terms have already become familiar, it is fair to assume that most would likely enter the political vocabulary by slow infiltration. In the following pages, I single out some of these terms that caught my attention and relate their *meaning,* the *context* of their coinage and/or usage *example*s.

A Mazruiana Glossary

ACTIVE INSTABILITY
A type of political instability that is characterized by rapid changes. Prediction in such a situation is particularly difficult. Institutions arise and collapse; men emerge and then are submerged, policies fluctuate.[1] See also IMMINENT INSTABILITY; LATENT INSTABILITY.

AFRABIA
A Mazruiana concept that links the languages, religions, and identities across both the Sahara Desert and the Red Sea in a historical fusion of Arabism and Africanity in the New World Order.² Mazrui maintained that although the concept is new, the notion is not. There is evidence of Arab settlements on the East African coast and in the Horn of Africa well before the birth of the Prophet Muhammad S. A. W. And the fact that the first great muezzin of Islam was Seyyidina Bilal is evidence that there was an African presence in Mecca and Medina that was pre-Islamic. Bilal was there before he was converted—a symbol of older Arabian link with Africa. AFRABIA is a pre-Hijriyya phenomenon.³

AFROSAXONS
One out of every five black men lives outside Africa. The great majority of those who are outside are in the Western Hemisphere. Some are now native speakers of Spanish, like the black Cubans. Some have grown up with the Portuguese language in the ghettos of Brazil. Still others are part of the French-speaking world scattered from Haiti to Martinique. There are also a few Arabic speakers in parts of the Middle East, but the largest single group outside of Africa is the Afro-Saxons - black people whose mother tongue is the English language. They include black Americans, Jamaicans, Trinidadians and, increasingly, black Britons and black Canadians.⁴

AGGRESSIVE DEPENDENCY
This reflects a rebellion against the dominant culture, but in a manner that betrays a lack of genuine self-confidence. Aggressive dependency sometimes denotes a profound lack of adequate social direction, an experience of anomie or alienation, yet with a clear target for one's grievances, a villain to blame for one's self-hatred.⁵
   See also SUBMISSIVE DEPENDENCY.

ANDROGYNIZATION OF THE STATE
One of the implications of the sacrilizing of the state in many societies. A process that seems to be diluting the patriarchal nature of the state. In other words, Mazrui suggested that if on the one hand the church is getting androgynized, and on the other hand the church and state are forging new links, the androgynization of the church helps the androgynization of the state.[6] See also SACRILIZING OF THE STATE; DENATIONALIZATION OF THE STATE.

AUTHORITATIVE PAN-SOCIALISM
A solidarity between two governments such as Communist China and Tanzania under Julius Nyerere. In this case, the relationship was not between the government of Communist China and an opposition in an African country. It was between one government and another, both influenced in varying degrees by socialistic values and radical perspectives.[7] See also DISSIDENT PAN-SOCIALISM.

BALANCED DEPENDENCY
Mazrui argued that non-alignment is one example of balanced dependency since it is based on the assumption that a client with more than one patron was freer than a uni-patronized dependent. A country that was heavily dependent on the USA, was less autonomous than a country that managed to get foreign aid both from the USA and the Soviet Union.[8]

BENEVOLENT RACISM
A racial paternalism and altruistic ethnocentrism that seeks to be of service to 'lower creatures.' It is a sense of racial superiority accompanied by readiness to be of service to the 'inferior.' It exploits its own resources to serve other groups.[9] Benevolent racism entails racial paternalism plus commitment of resources and readiness to sacrifice.[10] See also BENIGN RACISM; MALIGNANT RACISM.

BENEVOLENT RECOLONIZATION
A type of Inter-African recolonization that benefits the weaker country more than the intervening one. One example is when Julius Nyerere of Tanzania invaded Uganda and had to push away the dictator that had been very damaging to Uganda. Benevolent intervention benefits the weaker country more than the intervening one.[11] See also BENIGN COLONIZATION; MALIGN COLONIZATION.

BENEVOLENT SEXISM
A form of discrimination that is protective, or generous, towards the otherwise underprivileged gender. Gallantry and chivalry in defense of a woman's honor is a form of benevolent sexism.[12] See also BENIGN SEXISM; MALIGNANT SEXISM.

BENIGN COLONIZATION
One type of Inter-African recolonization when the moral plusses and minuses even out—a balanced moral budget. For instance, there was the annexation of Zanzibar by Tanganyika in 1964. Nobody consulted the people of Zanzibar whether they wanted to give up their sovereignty, whether they wanted to relinquish their seat at the UN, or whether they wanted to become a mere province of a country. But a dictator called Abeid Karume signed some document with Julius Nyerere, and the sovereignty of Zanzibar ended. The island was incorporated to the United Republic of Tanzania. Although Zanzibar was colonized, and it was a forced marriage with Tanganyika, it was a very generous marriage. It was also a marriage to a more stable partner. What it means is that small Zanzibar has disproportionate representation in the national institutions of the united country.[13] See also BENEVOLENT COLONIZATION; MALIGN COLONIZATION.

BENIGN RACISM
This is racial ethnocentrism without aggression. It is condescending

towards other groups without being malicious. It is sometimes race consciousness on the *defensive*—what Leopold Sengor called 'anti-racist racism.' It is self-reliant.'[14] Benign racism involves patronizing minorities without too much sacrifice in their favor.[15] See also BENEVOLENT RACISM; MALIGNANT RACISM.

BENIGN SEXISM
In the case of benign sexism the dominant gender is not being gallant and chivalrous to the disadvantaged gender (as when women and children are rescued first from a sinking ship). In its purest form, benign sexism acknowledges gender differences without bestowing sexual advantage or inflicting a gender cost. Benign sexism is harmless sexism.[16] See also BENOVOLENT SEXISM; MALIGNANT SEXISM.

BI-RACIAL SLAVERY
One of the three types of slave systems that are the most intrinsically exploitative, and are characterized by a white master and black slaves.[17] See also UNIRACIAL SLAVERY; MULTIRACIAL SLAVERY.

BLACK ORIENTALISM
The coinage of this concept, or more precisely, the adaptation of Edward Said's terminology, took place in 2000 after the airing of a television series by Harvard Professor Henry Louis Gates, *Wonders of the African World*. Mazrui, who had himself earlier hosted a television documentary on the same subject, registered his negative reaction to the series by Gates as follows: 'Edward Said, the brilliant Palestinian Professor at Columbia University, made his mark when he published his book ORIENTALISM referring to the strange combination of cultural condescension, paternalistic possessiveness, and ulterior selectivity shown by certain Western scholars towards non-Western societies in Asia, 'the Middle East' and Africa. Indeed the concept of the Middle East that is so Euro centric, was itself born out of Orientalism. The

question that has been raised by Skip Gates' television series is whether it signifies the birth of Black Orientalism. Are we witnessing the birth of a new Black paradigm that combines cultural condescension with paternalistic possessiveness and ulterior selectivity? The condescension in Gates' television series might have been at its worst in Ethiopia and over the Ark of the Covenant. The paternalistic possessiveness was in Great Zimbabwe and in the wonders of the manuscripts in Timbuktu. The selectivity not only knocked out virtually the whole of North Africa; it has also knocked out Nigeria, Africa's most populous country.[18]

CALCULUS-FRIENDLY CULTURE
(At ease with mathematics). One of the two forms of culture that are responsive to the computer and the Internet. In the United States there is increasing evidence that immigrants from South Asia (especially India and perhaps Pakistan) have responded faster to the computer culture than most other Americans. On American campuses there is indeed evidence that Korean-American students seem to be more calculus-friendly than Italian-American students, and Jewish-American students seem to be more at ease with the digital revolution than African-American students. The opposite of calculus-friendly culture is calculus-challenged culture.[19]

CLANOCRACY
The system of politics in present-day Somalia after the collapse of the state into clan-conflicts. The Somali are now scouting around in clans. Their country is no longer a state but a clanocracy—rule by clan.[20]

COMBATIVE MARTYRDOM
One of the two forms of martyrdom in which one can use one's very disadvantage as a weapon of confrontation.[21]
See also SIBMISSIVE MARTYRDOM.

COMPREHENSIVE GLOBALIZATION
One of the three forms of globalization. Comprehensive globalization results from all the forces that are turning the world into a global village-compressing distance, homogenizing culture, accelerating mobility, and reducing the relevance of political borders. Under this comprehensive definition, globalization is the gradual villagization of the world.[22] See ECONOMIC GLOBALIZATION; INFORMATIONAL GLOBALIZATION.

CONTINENTAL JURISDICTION
Represents the assertion that there are certain African problems that should only be solved by Africans themselves, by the members of the Organization of African Unity.[23]

CREATIVE ECCLECTICISM
An intellectual approach that implies a genius for selectivity, for synthesizing disparate elements, and for ultimate independent growth in the intellectual field.[24]

CRIPPLED CAPITALISM
This is the kind of capitalism — introduced to Africa by British imperialism — with such characteristics as the borrowing of only certain sections of the Western ideology; the missing out of important balancing elements, which then reduce the efficacy of the borrowed mode. For example, Africans have been better at learning Europe's consumption patterns than at learning its production techniques; better at learning European tastes than European capacities; better at inheriting the profit motive from the peoples of capitalism than the entrepreneurial skills; better at learning to be acquisitive without being disciplined. Crippled capitalism, therefore, sometimes exaggerates the ills of capitalism in Africa. It is an inheritance that is lopsided. It may have been accidentally lopsided, or it may have been purposely lopsided. What is clear is

that it is not working in a balanced form.[25]

CULTURAL DEPENDENCY
This form of dependency affects values, tastes, skills and ideas. In Africa two types of institutions have been particularly important in their cultural consequences: churches and multinationals. As instruments for the dissemination of Western culture, churches and multinationals have been almost in a class by themselves. Of course, churches are active in promoting religious values, but they also inculcate a variety of other values because they still play a major role in the educational system. See also STRUCTURAL DEPENDENCY.[26]

CULTURAL ENGINEERING
This is a concept born out of a successful inter-marriage of the ideas of cultural management and social engineering and is defined as the deliberate manipulation of cultural factors for purposes of deflecting human habit in the direction of new and perhaps constructive endeavors. Sometimes the effort consists in changing cultural patterns enough to make it possible for certain institutions to survive. At other times the purpose of cultural reform is basically attitudinal change.[27]

CULTURAL RELATIVISM
One of the three forces that contradict the pretension of the Western culture to universalism. Under cultural relativism, cultures differ across space—from society to society. The moral distance between the West and Islam or between Africa and the West is narrower than often assumed. In the same vein, what are regarded as medieval aspects of African culture may have been shared by Western culture until relatively recently.[28] Also see EMPRICAL RELATIVISM; HISTORICAL RELATIVISM.

CULTURAL RETRIBALIZATION
This is an emerging new phenomenon. As we witness the enlargement of economic scale in the world, we are also witnessing cultural revivalism that ranges from the collapse of the Soviet Union, the disintegration of Yugoslavia, the rise of Hindu nationalism, the ferocity of the Palestinian intifada, and major ethnic conflicts in Africa.[29]

CULTURAL TREASON
A concept used to describe the attitude of Muslims in regard to the publication of Salman Rushdie's Satanic Verses. As Mazrui explains: Salman Rushdie has been perceived by many Muslims as being guilty of cultural treason for writing *The Satanic Verses*. They claim that Rushdie has not merely rejected or disagreed with Islam: almost unanimously Muslims who have read the book have concluded that Rushdie has abused Islam. They were further outraged by the fact that he had been lionized, praised, and lavishly rewarded and financed by enemies and critics of Islam.[30]

DEFENSIVE FANATICISM
While submissive fatalism might encourage acceptance and peaceful conformity, defensive fanaticism could generate rebellion. It was Muhammed Ahmed el-Mahdi who revealed his own potential in the realms of defensive fanaticism. He was the precursor of Sudanese nationalism, rallying religion behind nationalistic causes, marrying piety to patriotism.[31] Also see SUBMISSIVE FATALISM.

DENATIONALIZATION OF THE STATE
Denotes the supra-nationalizing and sub-nationalizing tendency of the state in our times. In Western Europe the state is getting supra nationalized on a macro-scale as European integration proceeds in fits and starts. On the other hand, Eastern Europe is getting ethnicized on a micro-scale at precisely the time when Western Europe is getting supra

nationalized on a macro-scale. While Western Europe struggles for the supra-state, Eastern Europe grapples with the implications of sub-states. Both trends are retreats from the Westphalian sovereign nation-state.[32] See also ANDROGYNIZATION OF THE STATE; RE-SACRILIZING OF THE STATE.

DIPLOMATIC COLD STORAGE

What Mazrui seemed to mean by this term is diplomatic isolation. This was how Mazrui used the term: As the fear of communism receded in the 1980s, the West felt freer to be tough about terrorism from the Muslim world. Libya was bombed. Syria was put into cold diplomatic storage....[33]

DISSIDENT PAN-SOCIALISM

Disguised socialistic ties between a Communist government and opposition groups in an African country. The moral, and to some extent material support the Chinese were extending to Kenyatta's government in Kenya, represented this form of pan-Socialism.[34] See also AUTHORITATIVE PAN-SOCIALISM.

DIVISION OF CONTROL

While the division of labor as a concept is familiar, division of control in society may be less clearly articulated. In Malaysia political power is overwhelmingly in the hands of the ethnic Malays, while economic leverage is disproportionately in the hands of the ethnic Chinese. What was the *de facto* deal struck between Blacks and whites after Nelson Mandela's release? In order to avert a racial war, the whites said to the Blacks: 'You take the crown, we shall keep the jewels.' The whites transferred political power to the Blacks but retained the bulk of economic control. The whites retained the best businesses, the best mines, the best jobs, and the best shops in the major cities. The Blacks acquired the power to govern within those constraints. The Blacks had received the political crown; the whites retained the economic jewels. Here again is a situation not of a division of labor but of a division of control—similar to the deal between ethnic Malays and ethnic Chinese in Malaysia.[35]

DUAL SOCIETY

A society whose fundamental divide is between two groups or between two geographical areas. The State in a dual society is vulnerable in a different way from the State in a plural society. In a dual society two ethnic groups may account for more than three quarters of the population.[36] See also PLURAL SOCIETY.

DUAL TYRANNY

This term, coined in 1975, denotes the situation of academic freedom, or the absence of it, in Africa. This was how Mazrui explained it: I believe intellectual freedom in Africa is up against dual tyranny. One—a domestic tyranny—the temptations of power facing those in authority at this particular stage of the history of our continent. This is the political tyranny of governments as yet insensitive to some of the needs of educational institutions. The other tyranny is to some extent external. It is the Euro centrism of academic culture as we know it today—the degree to which the whole tradition of universities is so thoroughly saturated with European values, perspectives, and orientations.[37]

ECONOMIC GLOBALIZATION

A form of glcbalization that stems from all the forces that are transforming the global market and creating new economic interdependencies across vast distances.[38]

See also COMPREHENSIVE GLOBALIZATION; INFORMATIONAL GLOBALIZATION.

ECUMENICAL STATE
One of the three models of the relationship between religion and politics in Africa, in which there is neither a state religion nor is the state completely separate from religious institutions. What distinguishes an ecumenical state is its readiness to accommodate the different religions through official institutions, or official processes, or both.[39] See also RELIGIOUS NATION; RELIGIOUS STATE.

ELECTRONIC THEOCRACY
A term coined in a disapproving reference to what Mazrui called the Christian near monopoly of religious programs on [Kenya's] electronic media.[40]

EMPIRICAL RELATIVISM
Empirical relativism has two aspects. One aspect concerns whether in practice Western civilization lives up to its own standards. The other concerns situations in which Western ethical standards are better implemented by other, non-Western civilizations.[41] See also CULTURAL RELATIVISM; HISTORICAL RELATIVISM.

ENSLAVING PHASE OF THE CLASH OF CIVILIZATION
One of the four phases of the clash of civilizations. At this phase, millions of Africans were exported to North, South, and Central America and to the Caribbean.[42] See also GENOCIDAL PHASE OF THE CLASH OF CIVILIZATION; IMPERIAL PHASE OF THE CLASH OF CIVILIZATION.

EVANGELICAL EXPLORATION
One of the three motivational types of exploration defined in terms of social purpose. Evangelical exploration is pursued by either secular or religious missionaries, and inspired by such goals as the spread of civilization, the suppression of the slave trade, or the propagation of a new creed.[43] See also EXPLOITATIVE EXPLORATION; SCIENTIFIC EX-

PLORATION.

EXPLOITATIVE EXPLORATION
One of the motivational types of exploration which is undertaken often for reasons of commerce, of exploring new markets or possible new sources of raw materials.[44]
See EVANGLICAL EXPLORATION; SCIENTIFIC EXPLORATION.

FACTUAL MEMORY
A kind of memory that is more familiar in our day-to-day lives—the retention in our minds of experiences, events and facts of the past.[45] Also see GENETIC MEMORY.

FEUDO-IMPERIAL INTERDEPENDENCE
One of the three stages of interdependence. Feudo-imperial interdependence is defined as a stage of interdependence that combines some of the characteristics of feudalism and some of the attributes of imperialism. A central characteristic of this kind of interdependence is hierarchy, and hierarchy is of course founded on the premise of inequality.[46]
See also MATURE INTERDEPENDENCE.

FORMAL IMPERIALISM
In much of the first half of the twentieth century, at least two-thirds of the Muslim world was lodged in the formal collective empire of the Western world. In the years of formal imperialism, and especially after the collapse of the Ottoman Empire, Muslim countries were colonies and dependencies of such countries as Britain, France, the Netherlands, and Italy. Although the British attempt to globalize formal empire was impressive, it fell far short of encompassing the world.[47] See also INFORMAL IMPERIALISM.

FRACTURED NATION-STATE

The African state is weak, perhaps, when class-consciousness is weak. Conversely, the nation is weak when ethnic consciousness is strong. So, weak class-consciousness weakens the state, and strong ethnic consciousness weakens the nation. The colonial state, for some reason, did not create classes for themselves (as Marx would have put it) but did help to create so-called tribes for themselves. So, the post-colonial scramble for scarce resources is not an inter-class struggle but an inter-ethnic struggle.[48]

FRANKENSTEIN STATE

A term coined in the context of a critique of the basic theoretical assumptions underlying Marxist and liberal attitudes to the state. Mazrui argued: What both ideologies have all too often overlooked is that the captives of the state are not only those on the receiving end of state oppression—those in power are also held hostage to the logic of the state. In other words, *whoever captures the state is captured by it.* The Frankenstein state asserts its logic. It overwhelms and sometimes devours its own creators.[49]

GENETIC MEMORY

One of the two forms of memory, that is connected with the usage genes. We shall never be forgotten as long as our genes survive in our descendants. This kind of remembering, when politicized, becomes the genealogical memory—the conscious tracing of descent and ancestry for reasons of sentiment, status, or stratification.[50] See also FACTUAL MEMORY.

GENOCIDAL PHASE OF THE CLASH OF CIVILIZATION

One of the four phases of the clash of civilizations. This was in the early years of the European migration and settlement of the Americas. Europeans clashed with civilizations like those of the Incas and Mayas

Paradigm Lost, Paradigm Regained

and effectively destroyed them.[51]
See also ENSLAVING PHASE OF THE CLASH OF CIVILIZATIONS; HEGEMONIC GLOBALIZATION; IMPERIAL PHASE OF THE CLASH OF CIVILIZATION.

GLOBAL AFRICA

Global Africa is simply defined as Africa and its interrelationship with its worldwide Diaspora.[52] It is a continent of Africa plus, firstly, the Diaspora of enslavement (descendants of survivors of the Middle passage) and secondly, the Diaspora of colonialism (the dispersal of Africans which continues to occur as a result of disruptions of colonization and its aftermath).[53]

GLOBAL APARTHEID

Mazrui used this term in his work titled, *Global Apartheid: Race and Religion in the New World Order*, and explained what it meant through a series of rhetorical questions: Is the white world closing ranks in Eastern Europe and the West? Will we see a more united, and potentially more prosperous, white world presiding over the fate of a fragmented and persistently indigent black world in the twenty-first century? Put in another way, now that apartheid in South Africa is disintegrating, is there global apartheid in the process of formation? With the end of the Cold War, is the white world closing ranks at the global level—in spite of current divisions within individual countries such as Yugoslavia? Is the danger particularly acute between black and white people? Just when we thought apartheid in South Africa was over, apartheid on a global scale is rearing its ugly head.[54]

GLOBAL PAN-AFRICANISM

One of the five levels of Pan-Africanism. Global Pan-Africanism brings together all the centers of black presence in the world, and adds the new black enclaves in Britain, France, and other European countries, which have come partly from the Caribbean and partly from the African continent itself. Potentially these black enclaves in Europe are the most radicalizable of them all because of a combination of their demographic smallness and economic weakness, and the fluctuations of the European economies themselves.[55] See also TRANS ATLANTIC PAN AFRICANISM; SUB-SAHARAN PAN AFRICANISM; TRANSSAHARAN PAN AFRICANISM; WEST HEMISPHERIC PAN AFRICANISM.

GLORIANA AFROCENTRICITY
One of the two types of Afrocentrcity that emphasizes the great and proud accomplishments of people of African ancestry—Africa at its most complex, Africa on a grand scale: the castle builders, those who built the walls of Zimbabwe or the castles of Gondar, or the sunken churches of Laibela.[56] See also PROLETERIANA AFROCENTRICITY.

HEGEMONIC GLOBALIZATION
The last of the four phases of the clash of civilizations. This stage is marked by economic globalization; information globalization (the Internet, computer, and information superhighway); and comprehensive globalization, or the villagization of the world.[57] See also ENSLAVING PHASE OF THE CLASH OF CIVILIZATIONS, GENOCIDAL PHASE OF THE CLASH OF CIVILIZATION; IMPERIAL PHASE OF THE CLASH OF CIVILIZATION.

HEGEMONIC HOMOGENIZATION
The dual consequences of globalization are homogenization and hegemonization. We are getting to be more and more alike across the world every decade. This increase of similarity is *homogenization*. The paradoxical concentration of power in a particular country or civilization is *hegemonization*. People dress more alike all over the world at the beginning of the twenty-first century than they did at the end of the nineteenth century (*homogenization*). But the dress code that is

being globalized is overwhelmingly the Western dress code (*hegemonization*). Today, the human race is closer to having world languages than it was in the nineteenth century (*Homogenization*)...but when we examine the languages that have been globalized, they are disproportionately European—especially English and French, and to a lesser extent, Spanish (*hegemonization*). At the beginning of the twenty-first century, we are closer to a world economy than we have ever been before in human history. A sneeze in Hong Kong, and certainly a cough in Tokyo, can send shock waves around the globe (*homogenization*).

And yet the powers that control this world economy are disproportionately Western. They are the G7: the United States, Japan, Germany, Britain, France, Canada and Italy, in that order of economic muscle (*hegemonization*). The Internet has now given us instant access to both information and mutual communication across long distances (*homogenization*). However, the nerve center of the global Internet is still located in the United States federal government (*hegemonization*).

Educational systems in the twenty-first century are becoming more and more alike across the world, with comparable term-units and semesters, and an increasing similarity of teaching structures and course content (*homogenization*). But the role models behind this dramatic academic convergence have been the educational systems of Europe and the United States, which have attracted both emulators and imitators (*hegemonization*). The ideological systems of the world in the twenty-first century are also converging as market economies seem to emerge triumphant.

Liberalization is being widely embraced, spontaneously or under duress. However, the people who are orchestrating and sometimes enforcing marketization, liberalization, and privatization are Western economic gurus, supported by the power of the World Bank, the IMF, the US, and the EU. Indeed, Europe is the mother of all modern ideologies, good and evil: liberalism, capitalism, socialism, Marxism, Fascism, Nazism, and others. The most triumphant by the end of the

twentieth century was Euro-liberal capitalism (*hegemonic homogenization*).[58]
See HEGEMONIZATION; HOMOGENIZATION.

HEGEMONIZATION
One of the two characteristics of globalization represented by the paradoxical concentration of power in a particular country or civilization. It is the emergence and consolidation of a hegemonic center. It is a disproportionate share of global power among a few countries.[59] See also HEGEMONIC HEGEMONIZATION; HOMOGENIZATION.

HISTORICAL RELATIVISM
One of the three notions that contradict the pretension of Western culture to universalism. Under historical relativism, cultures differ across time—from epoch to epoch or age to age. From the perspective of historical relativism, what was valid in the West at the beginning of the twentieth century is not necessarily valid in the West at the beginning of the twenty-first century. If validity is changeable in the West itself from generation to generation, how can the claim to universalism be sustained?[60] See also CULTURAL RELATIVISM; EMPIRICAL RELATIVISM.

HOMOGENIZATION
One of the two characteristics of globalization. We are beginning to resemble each other to a much greater degree than we ever did in the past, regardless of physical distance. Homogenization is increasing similarity—the process of expanding homogeneity.[61] See also HEGEMONIC HOMOGENIZATION; HEGEMONIZATION.

HORIZONTAL(NUCLEAR) PROLIFERATION
One of the two sources of the danger of nuclear war. The involvement of new members in the nuclear club—more countries in the nuclear

war game. The NPT was in fact intended to deal with both the risk of vertical proliferation among the great powers and the horizontal addition of new nuclear powers.[62] See also VERTICAL PROLIFERATION.

HORIZONTAL INTEGRATION
One of the strategies in the fight against dependency. This involves not only *national* integration within each country but regional integration within each country as well. Pan-Africanism therefore becomes an instrument of horizontal integration.[63]

IMMINENT INSTABILITY
A situation where change and turbulence are expected at any time; and yet no such change or disruption takes place. Many Black African countries have an air of imminent instability even when the regime in power appears to be in full control. The instability is imminent when one is not surprised to hear of a military coup or a similar upheaval from one day to the next; and yet the air of instability continues. For the forecaster, such a situation is caught between the assurance of continuity and the imminence of sudden change.[64] See also ACTIVE INSTABILITY; LATENT INSTABILITY.

IMPERIAL (PHASE OF THE) CLASH OF CIVILIZATION
One of the four phases of the clash of civilizations. During this phase the West colonized or semi-colonized more than three quarters of the globe. Westerners settled in some parts of the world, governed in others, and controlled wherever they could.[65] See also ENSLAVING PHASE OF THE CLASH OF CIVILIZATION, GENOCIDAL PHASE OF THE CLASH OF CIVILIZATION; HEGEMONIC GLOBALIZATION.

IMPERIAL RECONSTITUTION
It involves a complete or partial resurrection of the same imperial power, recently dethroned.[66] See also IMPERIAL REINCARNATION.

IMPERIAL REINCARNATION

It is a perceived transmigration of the 'soul' of empire from one center to another emphatic center, usually a relative. The idea of a special relationship between [Britain and the United States] has been cultivated, especially by London. Although the British have not given up all diplomatic independence in their dealings with Muslim world, a cornerstone of British policy has been to support American goals as much as possible. The policy included pro-Iraqi policies during the Iran-Iraq war; anti-Iraqi policies in the 1990s; collaboration with US military and political decisions regarding Libya; and unwavering loyalty to US insistence on continued UN sanctions against Iraq, long after the end of Operation Desert Storm. The two Anglo-Saxon powers have each used the United Nations to lend legitimacy to the reincarnation of Pax-Britanica as Pax-Americana...

The global empire that the British attempted in the formal sense has been carried further by the Americans, in an informal manner; with imperial sanctions against dissidents, the imperial soul has transmigrated.[67] See also IMPERIAL RECONSTITUTION.

INFORMAL IMPERIALISM

In much of the second-half of the twentieth century, most of the Muslim world has existed within the informal collective empire of the West. In the more recent years of informal imperialism, the United States has assumed a preeminent hegemonic position, supported by two or three of the major European powers...It is the United State's informal empire [rather than the formal empire of the British] that much more closely approaches real global scale. But the United States does not act alone. It is a global imperial power with sub-imperial lieutenants: Britain and France in global political affairs, and Germany and Japan in global economic affairs.[68] See also FORMAL IMPERIALISM.

INFORMATIONAL GLOBALIZATION

A form of globalization which stems from all the forces which are exploding into the information highway - expanding access to data and mobilizing the computer and the Internet into global communication.[69] See also COMPREHENSIVE GLOBALIZATION; ECONOMIC GLOBALIZATION.

INTEGRATED CLEAVAGE

This is the disturbing anomaly concerning the tensions of social nearness in horizontal relationships.[70] Mazrui coined this term in reference to the tension...between an Arab population in Zanzibar which had acquired Swahili as its mother tongue and become substantially Africanized in certain aspects of culture, on one side, and then on the other, the Africans of Zanzibar who also spoke Swahili as their mother tongue, who also accepted Islam as their religion, and who had acquired certain aspects of the Arab lifestyle, but who still considered themselves as a group apart.[71]

INTELLECTUAL ACCULTURATION

This is a concept that need not be confused with ideological conversion. A pro-Western African could cease to be pro-Western tomorrow if he suddenly discovered something shockingly evil about a particular Western policy. Ideological conversion is a more superficial state of mind than intellectual acculturation. To be in favor of this country or that, and to be attracted by this system of values rather than that, are forms of ideological conversion. Under a strong stimulus one can change one's creed, but it is much more difficult to change the process of reasoning which one acquires from one's total educational background. No amount of radicalism in a Western-trained person can eliminate the Western style of analysis that he acquires.[72]

INTER-AFRICAN RECOLONIZATION

This involves stronger African states taking over weaker African states that collapsed, and putting them under a sound African footing politically.[73] See also BENOVOLENT RECOLONIZATION; BENIGN COLONIZATION; MALIGN COLONIZATION.

INTIMIDATORY LEADER

One of the four types of leadership in Africa. This type of leader relies primarily on fear and on instruments of coercion to assert his authority. All leaders have to use some degree of force, but the intimidatory leader specializes in it.[74] See also MOBILIZATION LEADER; LEADER OF RECONCILIATION; PATRIARCHAL LEADER.

LATENT INSTABILITY

One of the three types of instability. At first latent instability looks very similar to imminent instability, and yet there are fundamental differences. While one would not have been surprised if the ruler of Zanzibar had been overthrown the week after he came to power, one would indeed be surprised if the Apartheid system of South Africa crumbled next week. In Zanzibar under Karume instability was imminent in that it could have happened at almost anytime, even if it did not happen for quite a long time. But in the South African racial system the instability is latent, and could be delayed for many years, and yet inherently within the system are the seeds of its own destruction.[75] See also ACTIVE INSTABILITY; IMMINENT INSTABILITY.

LEADER OF RECONCILIATION

One of the four types of leadership in Africa. This type of leader relies for his effectiveness on qualities of tactical accommodation and a capacity to discover areas of compromise between otherwise antagonistic viewpoints. He remains in control for as long as he is successful in the politics of compromise and synthesis. The reconciliation is quite of-

Paradigm Lost, Paradigm Regained 157

ten between antagonistic political interest groups. But in present-day Africa the reconciliation leader may have to perfect also the art of reconciling the military with the civilian sectors of authority.[76] See also INTIMIDATORY LEADER, MOBILIZATION LEADER; PATRIARCHAL LEADER.

LENINIST CZAR

This is a term coined in 1966 in reference to Mazrui's claim that Kwame Nkrumah, the first leader of independent Ghana, shared certain features with Lenin and Czar. Mazrui's substantiated his hypothesis as follows. There is little doubt that, quite consciously, Nkrumah saw himself as an African Lenin. He wanted to go down in history as a major political theorist—and he wanted a particular stream of thought to bear his own name. Hence the term Nkrumahism- a name for an ideology that he hoped would assume the same historic and revolutionary status as 'Leninism.' The fountain-head of both Nkrumahism and Leninism was to remain Marxism—but these two streams that flowed from Marx were to have a historic significance in their own right. But while Nkrumah strived to be Africa's Lenin, he also sought to become Ghana's Czar. Nor is Nkrumah's Czarism necessarily 'the worse side' of his personality and behavior. On the contrary, his Czarism could—in moderation—have mitigated some of the harshness of Leninism. It is even arguable that a Leninist Czar was what a country like Ghana needed for a while. Nkrumah's tragedy was tragedy of *excess*, rather than of contradiction. He tried to be too much of a revolutionary monarch.[77]

LUMPEN MILITARIAT

The term was coined in the context of a discussion of the first military coup in Africa, the overthrow in 1971 of the Obote government by Idi Amin in Uganda. Mazrui defined a lumpen militariat as an army that is under-professionalized. An internalization of professional norms, and adherence to a professional ethic, a readiness to submit with pride to a professional discipline—these are qualities still underdeveloped [in Uganda]. In such a situation, the assumption of political power carries the risk of the further de-professionalization of the army.'[78]

MACRORETRIBALIZATION
One of the two forms of primordial retribalization that have re-emerged since the end of the Cold War. Western Europe shows strides in regional integration despite hiccups as the 1992 referendum in Denmark against the Mastricht Treaty. Regional integration can be *macroretribalization* if it is race-conscious. Macroretribalization can be the solidarity of white people, an arrogant pan-Europeanism greater in ambition than anything seen since the Holy Roman Empire.[79] The decline of socialist ideology throughout Eastern Europe is accompanied by a resurgence of primordial culture. Marxism has either died or been de-Leninized, but a pan-European identity is reasserting itself on a scale greater than the Holy Roman Empire.[80]
See also MICROTRIBALIZATION.

MACROSEGREGATION
The creation of separate monoracial and unicultural 'homelands' for [different] groups.[81] See also MICROSEGREGATION.

MALIGNANT COLONIZATION
One of the three forms of inter-African recolonization in which the main beneficiary becomes the powerful country. Benevolent colonization benefits the weaker; benign colonization benefits both countries equally, morally and materially. Malignant colonization benefits mainly the powerful country. This applies to Ethiopia under Haile Selassie eating up Eritrea in 1962. Perhaps it applies to Morocco and its absorbing Western Sahara. Outside Africa, it applies to Indonesia's absorption of East Timor. All these three cases are examples of

Paradigm Lost, Paradigm Regained 159

recolonization gone malignant.[82] See also BENOVOLENT RECOLONIZATION; BENIGN COLONIZATION.

MALIGNANT RACISM

A racial hostility or contempt toward others. It carries *malice* toward others. Malignant racism is basically racism on the *offensive* [and] is often exploitative of other groups.[83] See also BENIGN RACISM; BENEVOLENT RACISM.

MALIGNANT SEXISM

The most pervasive and most insidious form of sexism. In most societies it subjects women to economic manipulation, sexual exploitation, and political marginalization.[84] See also BENIGN SEXISM; BENEVOLENT SEXISM.

MARTYRDOM COMPLEX

The concept was coined in relation to an examination of the Boer nationalism (Apartheid) and Jewish nationalism (Zionism). The martyrdom complex in Jewish experience has had varied manifestations across the centuries, going back to the myth of the exodus from Egypt. But the martyrdom complex found a more compelling expression after the ghastly genocidal horrors and obscenities of Hitler's concentration camps. Hitler was at once the greatest enemy of the Jews in history and the greatest (if unconscious) friend of the concept of 'Israel.' The horrors he perpetrated resulted in a great boost for the Zionist movement. Western Jews who had previously had reservations about the movement, were now more firmly converted...Afrikaner nationalism has a martyrdom complex of its own with the British in the role of German Nazi. The Dutch had colonized South Africa before the British. British imperialism later on compelled Afrikaners to vacate some of their settlements and trek north in 1835. This trek was the equivalent of their exodus — a major symbolic event in Afrikaner mythology...⁸⁵

MATURE INTERDEPENDENCE

The last of the three stages of interdependence. Mature interdependence combines sophistication with symmetry. The sophistication comes from enhanced technological capabilities and expanded social and intellectual awareness; the symmetry emerges out of a new egalitarian morality combined with a more balanced capacity for mutual harm. The different parties must not only need each other, but their different needs ought to be on a scale that makes possible serious mutual dislocations in case of conflict. The combination of an egalitarian ethic and reciprocal vulnerability, within the framework of wider technological and intellectual frontiers, provides the essence of mature interdependence.'[86]

See FEUDO-IMPERIAL INTERDEPENDENCE; PRIMITIVE INTERDEPENDENCE.

MICRORETRIBALIZATION

One of the two forms of retribalization that re-emerged in Europe in the post-Cold War period. In Eastern Europe microretribalization is particularly strong. Microretribalization is concerned with microethnicity, involving such conflicts as Serbians versus Croats, Russians versus Ukrainians, and Czechs versus Slovaks.[87]

See also MACRO RE-TRIBALIZATION.

MICRO-SEGREGATION

This is the separation of races in towns and localities.[88] See also MACRO-SEGREGATION.

MILITARY DEMOCRACY

This signified a system of conflict management in the pre-colonial/pre-independent Africa. Mazrui explains this concept as follows. With the coming of the rifle in the colonial Africa, and the tank in independent Africa, military elitism assumed sharper differentiation. The old days of military democracy, when everyone passed through the warrior stage, and the weapons were simple ones capable of being manufactured by the warrior himself, were now replaced by the era of military professional specialists, with weapons requiring high technological skill to manufacture, and some specialized training to use.[89]

MILITARY THEOCRACY
A concept developed in reference to Idi Amin's moves in the direction of creating an ecumenical state in Uganda, in which the government was neither religiously neutral nor religiously monopolistic, but capable of serving as a referee among contending denominations.[90] This concept is based on an earlier discussion in which Mazrui raises the question of whether Uganda has under Idi Amin been evolving in to a military theocracy considering state sponsorship of religious ceremonies, the banning of mini-skirts, newly-imposed drinking hours, a ban on certain kinds of 'teenage dancing,' and the enforcement of religious unity.[91]

MOBILIZATION LEADER
One of the four kinds of leadership in Africa. This type of leader tends to be activated more by ideological factors than do the other three kinds of leaders. He also needs personal charismatic qualities more than do the other three, though these other kinds of leaders may combine charisma with their other qualities.[92] See also INTIMIDATORY LEADER; LEADER OF RECONCILIATION; PATRIARCHAL LEADER.

MULTIRACIAL SLAVERY
One of the three forms of slave systems in which both master and slave could be of any race or color.[93] See also BI-RACIAL SLAVERY; UNIRACIAL SLAVERY.

NUCLEAR APARTHEID
A situation involving five Nuclear Haves, who are under no special pressure to give up their own weapons of mass destruction, and many nuclear Have-Nots who are punished when they presume to go nuclear or build arsenal of mass destruction.[94]

PAN-PIGMENTATIONALISM
This is affinity of color. Afro-Asianism had been solidarity of a shared humiliation, as *colored people*. Colonialism was only one form that this humiliation took. The participants at the Bandung Conference of Non-Aligned States were not all former colonies. China was no more a former colony of a western power than Guatemala was a former colony of the United States. The credentials for participation at Bandung were therefore not a shared experience of colonial annexation but a shared quality of being 'Afro-Asian.' And the ultimate bond between Asians and Africans was, at least in the political climate of that time, the quality of being *non-white*.[95]

PATRIARCHAL LEADER
This is a type of leader, who may be interventionist or permissive, and commands neo-filial reverence as a real father figure. The permissive patriarchal leader prefers to withdraw from involvement in the affairs of the nation and dominate the scene from a god-like position in the background rather than as a participating politician. There may be occasions when he has to intervene actively in determining the direction of national change, but in general his style is that of delegation to his lesser colleagues who carry out the day-to-day business of guiding the nation. A patriarchal leader with a permissive style intervenes only when his colleagues are unequal to a particular emergency or crisis, or when the younger members of his national family are quarreling among themselves.[96] See also INTIMIDATORY LEADER; MOBILIZING LEADER;

LEADER OF RECONCILIATION.

PAX-AFRICANA

This is a system of peacemaking, peace enforcement and collective security for Africa and by Africans themselves.[97] Mazrui coined the term in his 1967 book, *Towards Pax Africana*. He then clarified it by stressing that the political ambition implied by this concept is not to impose an African peace on *others*—that would indeed be ambitious. The word 'Africana' in this concept describes both the nationality of the pace-makers and the continental limits of their jurisdiction, for *Pax Africana* asserts that the peace of *Africa* is to be assured by the exertions of *Africans* themselves. The idea of a 'Pax Africana' is the specifically military aspect of the principle of continental jurisdiction.[98] In his 1980 BBC Reith Lectures, however, Mazrui broadened the meaning of the concept to the extent he was unprepared to do in 1967. In this lecture, he said, I would like to carry my concept of *Pax Africana* one stage further. It is not enough that Africa should have a capacity to police itself. It is also vital that Africa should contribute effectively towards policing the rest of the world. It is not enough that Africa should find the will to be peaceful with itself; it is also vital that Africa should play a part in pacifying the world.[99]

PAX-HUMANA

Mazrui coined this term in the context of his argument that Africa's effect on the stability of the world, if any, seems to be a *disturbing one*. However, Africa has also been edging the world towards a concept of *Pax Humana* in three ways. There is, first, Africa's impact on the development of international law. Then there is African involvement in the evolution of international instruments of coercion under the United Nations. Third, and perhaps the most paradoxical of all, is Africa's role in the erosion of the principle of 'national sovereignty' as the basis of international relations.[100]

PIGMENTATIONAL SELF-DETERMINATION

This concept was coined in the context of the analysis of nationalism in Africa. On the early days of African nationalist movements, Mazrui argued, some form of collective identity had to be present if it was to be 'nationalism' at all. The group identity at the beginning of African nationalism was the identity of blackness racially, which is connected with the only sense of 'self-determination' that has been present in African nationalism all along—a kind of implied *pigmentational self-determination*. According to Mazrui, Kwame Nkrumah once framed the case in the following terms: 'The problem of Africa, looked at as the whole, is a wide and diversified one. But its true solution lies in the application of one principle, namely, the right of people to rule themselves. But what is *people*? Nkrumah does not seem interested in a precise definition. For him there is at least one kind of situation where foreign rule is conspicuous—and that is when the rulers are white and the ruled are evidently a different color.'[101]

PLURAL SOCIETY

A society that has a multiplicity of ethnic groups. In other words, it is a sociologically diverse society combined with a plurality of political allegiances. See also DUAL SOCIETY.[102]

POLITICAL HYGIENE

Julius Nyerere was convinced that politics has a great potential for being a dirty game. To him what can so easily make politics dirty is precisely what Western intellectuals have often jealously valued –the multi-party structure of competition for power… Nyerere argued that political honesty and party politics of the Western style are often in a state of tense incompatibility. When in 1965 Tanzania experimented with competitive elections within a single party structure, the motivation was, therefore, to some extent, political hygiene.[103] If dirt in politics was to be avoided, it was essential to avoid the conditions that give

Paradigm Lost, Paradigm Regained 165

rise to it. Preeminent among those conditions is the inter-party political contest. It was far healthier to devise elections in which members of the same party competed for office. In many elections the Party itself would be in a better position to control the degree of mutual mud-slinging that its members were to be permitted to indulge in.[104]

POLITICAL METREOLOGY
It is a scientific attempt to discern the interaction between social forces in specific societies and the resultant trend in the political atmosphere.[105]

POLITICAL NOSTALGIA
A phenomenon that arises almost by definition from an idealization of the political past.[106]

POLITICAL RE-TRADITIONALIZATION
Represents concrete attempts to formulate policies either from the influence of indigenous mores or in pursuit of ends defined according to indigenous criteria.[107]

POLITICAL SUPERANNUATION
This is a special case of occupational transferability. The latter may involve changing jobs between, say, diplomacy and academic life, or between the legal profession and the manufacturing enterprise. However, political superannuation is a process by which those who hold public office are permitted to save, invest, or create alternative occupational cushioning should they be thrown out of office in the days ahead. Political superannuation is an insurance policy against the political rainy day.[108]

PRIMITIVE INTERDEPENDENCE
One of the three stages of interdependence. Primitive interdependence

is defined as the cooperative relationship that exists in conditions of rudimentary technology and limited social horizons.[109] See also FEUDO-IMPERIAL; INTERDEPENDENCE; MATURE INTERDEPENDENCE.

PRIMORDIAL SOCIALISM
Has been discovered in many different cultures and societies. It is usually accompanied by simpler forms of technology, kinship-related collectivism, a greater egalitarianism than so far has been achieved in any modern revolutionary society, and communal forms of property and land tenure.[110] See also REVOLUTIONARY SOCIALISM.

PROLETERIANA AFROCENTRICITY
This is one of the two types of Afrocentricity. Proleteriana Afrocentricity emphasizes the sweat of Africa's brow, the captured African as a co-builder of modern civilization. The enslaved as creator, the slave as innovator. Slave labor building or helping to build the Industrial Revolution in the Western world. Slave labor for better or for worse, helping to fuel the capitalist transformation in the Northern Hemisphere. The colonized peoples, both as victims, and as builders of the industrialized modern world. The resources of Africa, the minerals of Africa, extracted from beneath our feet, have been used for factories that have transformed the nature of the 20th century. Without those minerals this century would have been vastly different.[111] See also GLORIANA AFROCENTRICITY.

RACIAL SOVEREIGNTY
Although we are forced at times to talk about 'self-government' as if it was a single principle, we should only do so in the awareness that there are at least five concepts of self-government involved in the politics of anti-colonialism. There is, first, self government as an absence of colonial rule; secondly, self-government as sovereign independence, with all its ramifications in relations with other countries; thirdly, self-

government as an internal management of internal affairs, including the maintenance of law and order, a matter which may have serious implications externally; fourthly, self-government in the liberal democratic sense as government supported 'by the will of the nation, substantially declared'; and fifthly, self-government as government by rulers manifestly belonging to the same race as the ruled. Ethnicity as a basis of legitimation in African nationalistic thought cannot be over emphasized. All the five concepts of self-government converge on it. It is this central point of contact between all the five concepts of self-government that we have called the principle of *racial sovereignty*.[112]

RELIGIOUS NATION
One of three models of the relationship between religion and politics in Africa. This represents a situation where a country is officially declared to be Christian or a Muslim. In this sense, Zambia in the 1990s had officially declared itself a "Christian nation."[113] See also ECUMENICAL STATE; RELIGIOUS STATE.

RELIGIOUS STATE
One the three models of relationship between religion and politics. Here state and religious institution are interlocked. Ethiopia before the revolution of 1974 was a religious state or a Christian theocracy in this sense. Sudan since 1983 has been another kind of theocracy— Islamic theocracy.[114] Elsewhere, Mazrui defined a theocracy as a political system that uses God as a point of reference for policy-making and makes God the focus of political morality. Political wisdom in a theocracy is ultimately divinely inspired. The world of politics and the world of religion in a theocracy are profoundly intertwined.[115] See also RELIGIOUS NATION; ECUMENICAL STATE.

RE-SACRILIZING OF THE STATE
This reflects the decline of atheism. Among the more 'heady' slogans

of the 1960s was the dictum 'God is dead.' Is the collapse of communism in Europe an epitaph on atheism? It is certainly an epitaph on state-atheism. Official Godlessness is dying in Eastern Europe, as God is allowed to run for election once again. What is more, He is winning out in many parts of the former atheistic Soviet and Serbian empires. There are similar patterns in Asia and Africa. On our return in the reverse evolution, are we slowly finding our way back to fundamental sacred linkage? Is the state in more and more countries in the process of being re-sacrilized?[116] See also ANDRROGYNIZATION OF THE STATE; DE-NATIONALIZATION OF THE STATE.

RESTORATIVE NOSTALGIA
When political nostalgia is restorative, it has not given up the past. It still clings to the idea that the idealized picture of years gone by is something that can be restored to life. It is a feeling that destiny has not ruled out a repetition of history.[117]

RETARDED SOCIALISM
The kind of socialism that was introduced (or some had attempted to introduce) to Africa in a context of a good normative climate but on a barren structures and barren sociological soil.[118]

REVOLUTIONARY SOCIALISM
A child of Western culture. This need not mean that all revolutions emanate from Western culture. Neither need it mean that all forms of socialism are to be traced to the impact Western civilization. It is also a combination of concepts—socialism and revolution—that are almost uniquely Western. See also **PRIMORDIAL SOCIALISM**.

ROMANTIC GLORIANA
A form of African cultural nationalism. Romantic Gloriana advocates

pride in the complex civilizations of ancient Africa.[119] See also ROMANTIC PRIMITIVISM.

ROMANTIC PRIMITIVISM
This is one of the two forms of African cultural nationalism. Romantic Primitivism advocates pride in the simplicity of rural African village life.[120] See also ROMANTIC GLORIANA

SACRED SUICIDE
A Creed that overemphasizes a non-violent approach to human disagreement tends to sharpen suicidal inclinations in its fanatics.[121]

SCIENTIFIC EXPLORATION
One of the three types of exploration. It is often sponsored by learned societies, and inspired by the scientific ideal of pushing the curtain of darkness further and further back.[122]
See also EVANGELICAL EXPLORATION; EXPLOITATIVE EXPLORATION.

SHARIACRACY
A state based on the Islamic law (Sharia). Mazrui used this term (perhaps not for the first time) in his reply to Wole Soyinka's reaction to Mazrui's critique of Henry Louis Gates' TV series *Wonders of the African World*.[123] In the reply, Mazrui had this to say to Soyinka: Since you are a non-Muslim Nigerian, you are understandably worried about the rise of SHARIA based state (SHARIA-CRACY) in one Northern state [of Nigeria] after another. But non-Yoruba Nigerians (and the Yoruba President of the country Olusegon Obasanjo) are equally worried about some of the activities of the Odua People's Congress (OPC) (ETHNOCRACY) in the South-West...Those of us who genuinely love Nigeria are indeed worried by both trends. Have you compared which trend so far is costing more lives—SHARIA-CRACY in the North vs. ETHNOCRACY in the South-West?

SINS OF COMMISSION
One of the three types of sin of the press in the age of HEGEMONIC GLOBALIZATION. This includes distortion of stories and damaging selectively.[124] See also SINS OF OMISSION; SINS OF SUBMISSION.

SINS OF OMMISSION
One of the three types of sin of the press in the age of HEGEMONIC GLOBALIZATION. The Taliban story generated *comparisons* with treatment of women in Saudi Arabia. That was fair enough. However, the gender issue in the Taliban story did not generate *contrasts* of positive Islamic images—such as the fact that Indonesia, Pakistan, Bangladesh and Turkey have each had a woman Head of Government long before the US, France, and Russia had a woman president or Germany had a woman Chancellor.[125] See also SINS OF COMMISSION; SINS OF SUBMISSION.

SINS OF SUBMISSION
One of the three types of sin of the press in the age of HEGEMONIC GLOBALIZATION. This sin is not submission to the dictates of the truth but to the warning of politicians or the demands of advertisers or censorship imposed by subscribers.[126] See also SINS OF COMISSION; SINS OF OMISSION.

STRUCTURAL DEPENDENCY
Economic structural dependency can be defined in terms of two major characteristics of relationships. One characteristic is a hierarchical division of labor, as contrasted with a horizontal division of labor. A hierarchical division is one in which some types of producers are higher up in the structure of advantage than others. A horizontal division of labor is a division among equals. If primary producers come from the Southern Hemisphere and industrialized powers are in the Northern Hemisphere and the exchange is unequal, this situation gives us pre-

Paradigm Lost, Paradigm Regained 171

cisely the model of hewers of wood and drawers of water. Related to this phenomenon, an aspect of economic dependency in the structural sense, is a form of penetration that is unbalanced or asymmetrical.[127] Also see CULTURAL DEPENDENCY.

SUBMISSIVE DEPENDENCY
This is one of the two forms of dependency. It signifies an excessive deference towards metropolitan standards, a keenness to imitate the dominant culture, and a compulsive subservience to the conquering civilization.[128]
See also AGGRESSIVE DEPENDENCY.

SUBMISSIVE FATALISM
This is a Hobbesian concept in Islamic statecraft, encouraging obedience to those who exercise authority, provided they do no violence to the principles that Muhammed advocated and God willed…submissive fatalism might encourage acceptance and peaceful conformity…It also represents a readiness to accept the inevitable.[129]

SUBMISSIVE MARTYRDOM
One of the two forms of martyrdom in which [o]ne accepts what comes, resigns oneself, even bravely, without resistance. Sometimes you can do it submissively as a mission. Some have interpreted Jesus' passion as a form of submission. That Jesus carried the cross on which He was to be crucified and that He did not resist. That is one general interpretation of Martyrdom.[130]
See also COMBATIVE MARTYRDOM.

SUB-SAHARAN PAN-AFRICANISM
One of the five levels of Pan-Africanism. SubSaharan Pan-African- ism limits itself to the unity of black people or black countries south of the

Sahara. It could take the form of sub-regional unification, like the East African Community or the experimental Economic Community of West African States. Or it could be a commitment to limit solidarity to black African countries, excluding both the Arab states and the black people of the Americas.[131]

See also GLOBAL PAN-AFRICANISM; TRANS ATLANTIC PAN AFRICANISM; TRANS SAHARAN PAN AFRICANISM; WEST HEMISPHERIC PAN AFRICANISM.

TANZAPHILIA
It is neither a disease nor an exotic flower. It is a political phenomenon. It is a romantic spell that Tanzania casts on so many of those who have been closely associated with her.[132] It is also an *ideological* commitment to the goals of self-reliance and egalitarianism. As an ideological commitment, it delves deep into *moral* responses.[133]

TECHNO-CULTURAL GAP
Refers to the gap between norms and techniques in relation to the Western heritage in Africa. This is also a reflection of a profound incongruency that lies at the heart of the imported educational system in Africa. The wrong Western values were being provided as an infrastructure for the set of Western skills introduced...[134]

THEORY OF REVERSE EVOLUTION
A meta-level Mazruian theory also known as the round-trip evolution. The notion starts from the premise that there was a time in human antiquity when there were no states, no classes, no racism, and when women could be priestesses, matriarchs, 'amazons' or even rulers. The concept of round-trip evolution is partly a marriage of Karl Marx's progression of historical materialism and the Greek myth of Sisyphus. Under round-trip evolution, the human species will ascend Mt. Development slowly across centuries, be shocked by the lava and other vol-

canic activity at the summit, and then slowly retrace its steps downwards. Such a stage is marked, among other things, with denationalization of the state, re-sacrilizing of the state, and androgynization of the state.[135]

TRANS-ATLANTIC PAN-AFRICANISM
Is the third level of pan-African solidarity, encompassing the people of the Black Diaspora in the Americas as well as of the African continent. One form of trans-Atlantic Pan-Africanism limits itself to black people and excludes the Arabs of North Africa. Under this version Afro-Canadians, Jamaicans, black Americans, black Brazilians and others find common cause with Nigerians, Zimbabweans, Namibians and Ugandans, but find little in common with Egyptians, Libyans and Algerians. However, there is another version of trans-Atlantic Pan-Africanism, under which Stokely Carmichael of the Black Diaspora was a hero in Algiers, and Colonel Gaddafy of Libya extends financial support to black Americans.[136] See also
  GLOBAL PAN-AFRICANISM; SUB SAHARAN PANAFRICANISM; TRANS SAHARAN PAN AFRICANISM; WEST HEMISPHERIC PAN AFRICANISM.

TRANS-CLASS MAN
This concept was used in the context of a critique of the 'theories of class analysis' which 'have tended to underestimate possibilities of dual or multiple class affiliation in the same person.'[137] Mazrui defined the trans-class man as the person who is compelled to belong to more than one class in a situation of great structural fluidity.[138]

TRANS-SAHARAN PAN-AFRICANISM
One of the five levels of Pan-Africanism. Trans-Saharan panAfricanism extends solidarity to those who share the African continent across the Sahara desert—the Arabs and Berbers of the North. Trans-Saharan Pan-Africanism insists on regarding the great desert as a symbolic bridge

rather than a divide, a route for caravans rather than a death-trap.[139] See also SUBSAHARAN PAN AFRICANISM; GLOBAL PAN AFRICANISM; TRANS-ATLANTIC PAN AFRICANISM; WEST HEMISPHERIC PAN AFRICANISM.

TRIBAL CONSERVATISM
A body of thought in Africa that rests on a cumulative consensus that links the past with the present and the future.[140]

TRIPLE HERITAGE
A collective name for the three factors which have exerted their influence upon the history of Africa. These factors are the indigenous, the Islamic, and the Western[141]

UHURU WORSHIP
It is a cult of independence that continues to affect the course of Africa's evolution in multiple ways. Behind it all is the impact of specific personalities—the heroes and the villains who left their mark on a continent.[142]

UNIRACIAL SLAVERY
One of the three forms of slavery in which both the slaves and the masters are of the same race or color, such as black slave black master.[143] See also BI-RACIAL SLAVERY; MULTIRACIAL SLAVERY.

USAMAPHILIA
The secret admiration Usama bin Laden definitely enjoys among the frustrated and desperate masses of those humiliated by either Israeli policies or American power and global reach.[144]

USAMAPHOBIA
The hate or fear of Usama bin Laden and what he stands for.[145]

VERTICAL (NUCLEAR) PROLIFERATION

One of the two sources of the danger of nuclear war. This form of proliferation involves greater sophistication and diversification of nuclear options and nuclear technology in the arsenals of the great powers. The same nuclear powers increase and diversify their destructive capabilities.[146] See also HORIZONTAL (NUCLEAR) PROLIFERATION.

WEST-HEMISPHERIC PAN-AFRICANISM

One of the five levels of pan-Africansim. West-hemispheric Pan-Africanism encompasses West Indians, black Americans, black Brazilians and other black people of the Western Hemisphere. Within this version of Pan-Africanism the strongest links so far have been between black Americans and English-speaking West Indians.[147]

See also GLOBAL PAN-AFRICANISM; SUB-SAHARAN PAN-AFRICANISM; TRANSATLANTIC PANAFRICANISM; TRANS-SAHARAN PAN-AFRICANISM.

---

1 Mazrui (1977d 11).
2 Mazrui (1992c 62).
3 Mazrui (1992c 53).
4 Mazrui (1977d 68). See also Mazrui (1975d: 76-77).
5 Mazrui (1975c: 470).
6 Mazrui (1999: 17-19).
7 Mazrui (1973c: 157).
8 Mazrui (1977d 6).
9 Mazrui (1991: 97).
10 Mazrui (1991 102).
11 Mazrui (1996a: 7).
12 Mazrui (1998a: 225).
13 Mazrui (1996a: 7-8).
14 Mazrui (1991 97).
15 Mazrui (1991 102).
16 Mazrui (1998a: 228).
17 Ufumaka (1994: 56).
18 Mazrui (2000d: 1).

19 Mazrui (2000d: 3-4).
20 Mazrui (1996a: 2).
21 Mazrui and White (1989: 185).
22 Mazrui (2000d: 1-2).
23 Mazrui (1967d: 118).
24 Mazrui (1975a: 465).
25 Mazrui (1983a: 206-207)
26 Mazrui (1980d: 87).
27 Mazrui (1972 : xv).
28 Mazrui (2001d: 33)
29 Mazrui (2000d: 1).
30 Mazrui (1990b: 118).
31 Mazrui (1984: 291-292).
32 Mazrui (1999: 9-10).
33 Mazrui (1994b: 523).
34 Mazrui (1973c: 156).
35 Mazrui (20002d: 5).
36 Mazrui (1995c: 28).
37 Mazrui (1975b: 393).
38 Mazrui (2000d: 1).
39 Mazrui (2000f: 40-41).
40 Mazrui (1993d : 93).
41 Mazrui (2001d: 38).
42 Mazrui (2002f: 2).
43 Mazrui (1969b: 663).
44 Mazrui (1969b: 663).
45 Mazrui (1992a: 134).
46 Mazrui (1980a: 64).
47 Mazrui (1996c: 218).
48 Mazrui (1983a : 209).
49 Mazrui (1996c: 55).
50 Mazrui (1992a: 134).
51 Mazrui (2002f: 2).
52 Mazrui (1997b: 192-193).
53 Mazrui (2000e: 18).
54 Mazrui (1994b: 521, 525).
55 Mazrui (1977d: 69).
56 Mazrui (1992b: 3).
57 Mazrui (2002f: 3).
58 Mazrui (2001d: 34-36).
59 Mazrui (1998d:3)
60 Mazrui (2001d: 33).
61 Mazrui (1998d: 3).

Paradigm Lost, Paradigm Regained

62 Mazrui (1981a: 17).
63 Mazrui (1996d: 11).
64 Mazrui (1977d: 11).
65 Mazrui (2002f: 3).
66 Mazrui (1996c: 219-220).
67 Mazrui (1996c: 219-220).
68 Mazrui (1996c: 218-219).
69 Mazrui (2000d: 1).
70 Mazrui (1973b: 110).
71 Mazrui (1973b: 109).
72 Mazrui (1972).
73 Mazrui (1996a: 7).
74 Mazrui (1970: 538).
75 Mazrui (1977d: 11).
76 Mazrui (1970: 538-539)
77 Mazrui (1967b: 113).
78 Mazrui (1973a: 9).
79 Mazrui (1994b: 521).
80 Mazrui (1994b: 528).
81 Mazrui (1983b: 75).
82 Mazrui (1996a:7-8).
83 Mazrui (1991: 97).
84 Mazrui (1998b: 231).
85 Mazrui (1968b: 79-80).
86 Mazrui (1980a: 64).
87 Mazrui (1994b: 251).
88 Mazrui (1983b: 75).
89 Mazrui (1973a: 3).
90 Mazrui (1976b: 35).
91 Mazrui (1974b: 106).
92 Mazrui (1970: 539).
93 Ufumaka (1994: 56).
94 Mazrui (1998e: 9-10).
95 Mazrui (1967d: 210-211).
96 Mazrui (1970: 533).
97 Mazrui (1997c: 197).
98 Mazrui (1967d: 203).
99 Mazrui (1980b: 113).
100 Mazrui (1967d: 231).
101 Mazrui (1967d: 14).
102 Mazrui (1995c: 28-29).
103 Mazrui (1967c: 30-31).
104 Mazrui (2002g: 16-17).

105 Mazrui (1969c: 181).
106 Mazrui (1981c: 1).
107 Mazrui (1980b:458).
108 Mazrui (1968b: 84).
109 Mazrui (1980a: 64).
110 Mazrui (1981b: 66-67).
111 Mazrui (1992b: 3-4).
112 Mazrui (1967d: 21-23).
113 Mazrui (2000f: 40).
114 Mazrui (2000f: 40).
115 Mazrui (1974a: 107).
116 Mazrui (1999: 16-17).
117 Mazrui (1981c: 1).
118 Mazrui (1983a: 207).
119 Mazrui (1990a: 158-159).
120 Mazrui (1990b: 159).
121 Mazrui (1969: 319).
122 Mazrui (1969b: 663).
123 Mazrui (2000: 8).
124 Mazrui (2002f: 2).
125 Mazrui (2002f: 3).
126 Mazrui (2002f: 4).
127 Mazrui (1980d: 85).
128 Mazrui (1975c: 469).
129 Mazrui (1984: 291-293).
130 Mazrui and White (1989: 185).
131 Mazrui (1977d: 68).
132 Mazrui (1969a: 255).
133 Mazrui (1967c: 31).
134 Mazrui (1978a: 24).
135 Mazrui (1999: 5-25).
136 Mazrui (1977d: 68-69).
137 Mazrui (1968b: 94).
138 Mazrui (1968b: 83).
139 Mazrui (1977d: 69).
140 Mazrui (2001: 102); Mazrui (1974a: 116).
141 Mazrui (1986a: 115).
142 Mazrui (1967b: ix).
143 Ufumaka (1994: 56).
144 Mazrui (2001e: 7).
145 Mazrui (2001e: 6).
146 Mazrui (1981a: 17).
147 Mazrui (1977d: 69).

8. Paradigm Lost, Paradigm Regained: A Conclusion

Against the background of the discussions in the preceding chapters, I conclude this book by making a brief comparison of Ibn Khaldun, the 14th century Afro-Muslim thinker, and Ali Mazrui. The comparison does, I hope, also sum up, but more explicitly, what I have said in the book. What I shall *not* attempt here is an in-depth comparison of the paradigms of the two thinkers. But such a systematic look at the ideas of these thinkers is, needless to say, neither unprofitable nor beyond the realm of possibility.

For my purpose here, I organize my discussion around the following questions. Is there a sense in which Mazrui could be regarded as the Ibn Khaldun of the twentieth century, the postmodern Ibn Khaldun? Is Mazrui a reincarnation of Ibn Khaldun in our own times? Can we regain the lost paradigm of Ibn Khaldun through the works of Ali A. Mazrui? My answer to all of the questions is yes. I shall do my best to substantiate this positive statement below, but first must come clarification of relevant key concepts.

Let me begin with Ibn Khaldun's own remark: "When a man comes to know a problem or be certain about a matter, he must openly state (his knowledge or his certainty)."[1] If Ibn Khaldun had suggested in this way that scholars/intellectuals should ask questions and re-examine ideas and assumptions that societies have accepted as self-evident truth, and if such an approach represents a line in a postmodernist thought (as our working definition of postmodernism, which was elaborated in chapter three, suggests), does it not logically follow that there is a sense in which Ibn Khaldun himself could be regarded as postmodern? And if the answer is yes, as logic dictates, then would there not be some redundancy in the phrase "Postmodern Ibn Khaldun?" The answer here is, not quite.

True, in the above sense, postmodernism could easily be associated with Ibn Khaldun. To say this is not incorrect any more than it would be incorrect to trace social constructivism to Thucydides.[2] In other words, Ibn Khaldun's methodological orientation does place him in the club of postmodernists. However, Ibn Khaldun is a postmodernist thinker only in the methodological sense. But he is a pre-modern postmodernist thinker.

For all the contention surrounding the concept of postmodernism, there seems to be a general consensus that only our time, and not the time of Ibn Khaldun, can truly be considered the postmodern moment. Whereas Ibn Khaldun is postmodernist in a methodological sense, one cannot describe him in these terms in a temporal sense. But Ali A. Mazrui is postmodernist in both senses. Rather than redundancy, therefore, an element of accuracy is added by referring to Ali Mazrui as "a Postmodern Ibn Khaldun."

Why, then, is Ali A. Mazrui not a modern Ibn Khaldun (rather than a postmodern one)? As modernity comes before postmodernity in the sequence of time, there is no postmodernity prior to modernity and there is no postmodernity without the latter. By modernity I mean the stage in which the complex forces of democracy, nationalism, and industrialization are at work. Even in this simple sense, it is hard to say precisely where or when postmodernity begins and where or when modernity ends; or whether they run a parallel course or crisscross one another or whether they run a parallel course, crisscross, and follow one another simultaneously. When I chose to describe Ali A. Mazrui as a postmodern Ibn Khaldun rather than a *modern* one, there is thus also a desire to stick to the conventional meaning of the term "postmodern" in the temporal sense, although I do realize that the emergence of the enigmatic concept marks not just a transition from one stage to another, but also a discursive transformation engendered by the distorting simplicity associated with the pre-modern/modern binarism.

Despite the passage of centuries since the time of Ibn Khaldun, his works are being highly appreciated as relevant to our times.[3] In this context, my core argument as well as the conclusion of the book is that, although more than 600 years separate Ibn Khaldun (1332-1406) and Ali Mazrui (1933-, the two thinkers share much in common. This is not of course to suggest that I know that there is a tie, blood or otherwise, between Mazrui and Ibn Khaldun. It is also unclear whether Ibn Khaldun has inspired Mazrui. The parallels are nevertheless interesting and, as I elaborate below, some of them are quite substantive.

One example of a readily visible parallel between the two is their enduring philosophical vigor and formidable intellectual achievement. As indicated above, to the extent that both thinkers grappled with assumptions and histories that societies had internalized, they are postmodernists in methodological sense. It is a fully recognized fact, as the discussions in the preceding chapters demonstrate, that in almost all of his academic publications and other intellectual outputs, what Mazrui does is ask questions in the sense advocated by Ibn Khaldun, and to ask them just as well. Ali A. Mazrui and Ibn Khaldun also share striking similarities in their respective biography; interest in cultural paradigm; thematic concern with emphases on macro-level studies of societies and civilizations and on metatheoretical issues; and interest in geography as the mother of history, but not necessarily its father; as well as mastery of style of expression. I shall elaborate below some of these similarities.

Like Ibn Khaldun, Mazrui is a descendant from a learned and prominent family background.[4] Mazrui lost his father at the tender age of 14. Ibn Khaldun lost both of his parents also at the early age of 17. Like Ibn Khaldun, Mazrui is an academic wanderer, both literally and metaphorically. Ibn Khaldun wandered from Tunis, to Morocco and then to Egypt, where he arrived at the age 50 and began to lecture in Al Azhar, the oldest Islamic institution of higher education in the world. Not only did Mazrui "travel" from place to place for academic purposes, he had also to "settle" in Uganda, rather than in Kenya where he was born, and lecture at Makerere University, the oldest institution of higher education in East Africa, before moving to the United States on a similar mission.[5] It is also interesting to note that Mazrui tells that if his father had not died while he was young, he would have almost certainly ended up at Al Azhar.[6] During this period, Mazrui has met or conversed with and in some cases forged a lasting friendship with many notable individuals. The names that have been mentioned in this regard are Martin Luther King, Sedar Senghor, Muamar Ghadafi, Idi Amin, Julius K. Nyerere, and many, many others. Such encounters have no doubt enhanced Mazrui's unique insights into the political world. Robert W. Cox, the noted critical thinker in IR, said this about Ibn Khaldun:

> As participant observer of politics, [Ibn Khaldun] had excellent opportunities to develop his judgment, with access to many of the prominent personalities of the time, both within the Arabic-Islamic world and beyond it. During his own career, Ibn Khaldun had personal encounters with Pedro the Cruel of Castile in Seville, and with the Mongol conqueror Tamerlane outside of Damascus.[7]

Both Mazrui and Ibn Khaldun were entrusted individually with the position of high honor outside their countries of birth. From Makerere to Michigan and then to Cornell and Binghamton and in between, Mazrui occupied some of the most coveted positions in the academia.[8] Despite the fact that he was a "foreigner," Ibn Khaldun had also been appointed by the Sultan in Egypt to serve as a judge, "…a post always aspired after by the local faqihs and ulama."[9]

N. J. Dawood has commented that Ibn Khaldun was "gifted with rare insight, enabling him to penetrate the essentials of accumulated knowledge."[10] Others have noted a dialectical mind behind the thought of Ibn Khaldun.[11] Like Ibn Khaldun, it has also been said that, Mazrui has a dialectical mind[12] and that he has the power "to x-ray ideas"—that is, to quickly notice and point out any internal contradictions and irrationality in an adversary's position or thesis.[13] Related to this is the harmony between some of the epistemological assumptions held by the two thinkers. Robert Cox has summed up one of the epistemologies of Ibn Khaldun as being the view that the development of a state contains the seeds of its own destruction.[14] Such assumptions are found in many Mazruiana works, most notably in his discussion of what he fittingly called *The Frankenstein State*.[15]

I have indicated in chapter two that compared to the major schools in contemporary IR, Mazruiana is farthest from neorealism. On Ibn Khaldun's work, this is what Robert Cox has to say in this respect: "There is little in common between Ibn Khaldun and our contemporary neorealism…There is much in common with the effort to conceive of post-Westphalian world…Ibn Khaldun may have something to say to those endeavoring to think in terms of post-globalization."[16]

Like the 14th century thinker, Mazrui has anticipated some of the concepts and theories in his field of interest, as outlined in chapter three. Ibn Khaldun works have won admiration from Arnold Toynbee, the renowned historian of the recent past to Robert Cox, the celebrated critical thinker in IR today. In fact, Cox even claimed: "Toynbee certainly borrowed from him some of his leading ideas, including the principle that physical environments must not be either too hard or too lush in order that they stimulate the development of civilization."[17] It is mentioned in the same text that: "Ernest Gellener considers Ibn Khaldun to be the best interpreter of Islamic society and a sociologist whose theoretical insights are comparable to those of Durkheim and Weber."[18]

The same author sees a similarity between what Hedley Bull's had called the normative principles of world order and what Ibn Khaldun had discussed under the rubric of the essential conditions of a civilization.[19] Similarly M. A. Enan says this about Ibn Khaldun: "It was believed that Western research was the first to discover the philosophy of history and principles of sociology and political economy, but it was then found that Ibn Khaldun had long preceded the West, and had treated those subjects in his Prolegomena, and expounded many of their principles with intelligence and vigor."[20]

Mazrui also shares with Ibn Khaldun linguistic sophistication and a high level of proficiency. In chapter four I dealt with aspects of the linguistic sophistication of Mazrui. In regard to Ibn Khaldun's works, one analyst has suggested that they "should be often read, not only to admire his marvelous thought and research, but also to learn from it the methods of expression of many social theories, which otherwise are difficult to express, because the Prolegomena of Ibn Khaldun is an inestimable wealth in the intellectual legacy of Arabic literature."[21] With the exception of the medium of writing—Mazrui writes in English—the same can be said about Mazruiana.

Ibn al-Khatib, one of the students of Ibn Khaldun, is also said to have remarked on the prose of his teacher, that it represented "channels of rhetoric, gardens of art, precious metals cleverly shaped, the prologues are similar to the epilogues in fertility of imagination and fluency of expression."[22]

Moreover, Mazrui shares with Ibn Khaldun a long-standing interest in ecological and geographical explanation of social behavior,[23] although the latter thinker spends more time on the impact of geography and ecology on societies than the former does. Ibn Khaldun's Chapter one of *The Muqadimmah* focuses on ecological determinism.[24]

Though not certainly to the extent of Ibn Khaldun's, some of Mazrui's ideas at times pose a challenge to the reader/listener on whether one ought to characterize him as a secular or a religious thinker.[25] In regard to Ibn Khaldun, Ahmed Akbar observed: "for all his 'scientific' objectivity—and for many Muslims it is excessive—Ibn Khaldun still writes as a believer.'"[26]

Last but not least, Ibn Khaldun and Mazrui share eclecticism as an intellectual approach of choice. Chapter one of this book has touched upon the eclecticism and interdisciplinary feature in Mazruiana. Similarly, Western researchers have long considered Ibn Khaldun "a philosopher, a historian of civilization, a scholar of sociology and political economy and moreover acknowledge him to be the first to treat these subject."[27] In fact, Ibn Khaldun himself had said: "The (writing of history) requires numerous sources and greatly varied knowledge. It also requires a good speculative mind and thoroughness."[28] Creative eclecticism and *reflection* also constitute the epistemological foundation of Mazruiana. PARADIGM LOST, PARADIGM REGAINED.

1 Ibn Khaldun (1967: 44).
2 See Lebow (2001: 547-559).
3 For why Ibn Khaldun is of interest today see for instance Cox (1992: 147).
4 See Mazrui (1989a: 472).
5 For the context see Nyang (1981).
6 See Mazrui (1973b); see also Mazrui (1989a).
7 Cox (1992: 147).
8 For reference to earlier part see Nyang (1981: 12-13).
9 Enan (1975: 69).
10 Ibn Khaldun (1967: vii).
11 Cox (1992: 153).
12 Alamin Mazrui (2001: 8).
13 Kokole (1998: 12).
14 Cox (1992: 154).
15 Mazrui (1996c).
16 Cox (1992: 148).
17 Cox (1992: 156, ft. 43).
18 Cox (1992: 156, ft. 43).
19 Cox (1992: 141).
20 Enan (1975: 152-153).
21 Enan (1975: vii).
22 Quoted in Enan (1975: 23).
23 See for instance Mazrui (1993c: 3); Mazrui (1969a: 183).
24 Ibn Khaldun (1967).
25 For a discussion of Ibn Khaldun in this regard, see Imam (1988).
26 Ahmed (2002: 6).
27 Enan (1975: 153).
28 Ibn Khaldun (1967: 15).

APPENDIX

SELECT HONORS AND TRIBUTES TO ALI A. MAZRUI
THE AMERICAN YEARS (1972 to the present)

Fellow, Center of Advanced Study in the Behavioral Sciences
Palo Alto, California (1972-1973).

Senior Fellow, Hoover Institution on War, Revolution and Peace
Stanford, California (1973-1974).

President, African Studies Association of the United States
(1978-1979).

Reith Lecturer, **"THE AFRICAN CONDITION"**
British Broadcasting Corporation (Radio World Service Series)
London, England (1979).

Vice President, International Congress of African Studies
(1979- 1991).

Vice President, Royal Africa Society
London, England (1980- present).

Honorary Fellow, Ghana Academy of Arts & Sciences
(from 1985).

Author and Narrator, **THE AFRICANS: A TRIPLE HERITAGE**
TV and video series and accompanying book (1986).

Andrew D. White Professor-at-Large
Cornell University
Ithaca, NY (1986-1992).

Albert Luthuli Professor-at-Large
University of Jos
Jos, Nigeria (1986 to present).

Member, College of Fellows of the International Association of Middle Eastern Studies
(1986 to present).

Nominated by the University of Bombay and Institute of Objective Studies, India, for inclusion in a list of one hundred greatest Muslim scholars of the twentieth century.

Faculty Achievement Award
The University of Michigan at Ann Arbor
Ann Arbor, Michigan (1988).

AFRICARE Distinguished Service Award
For outstanding contribution to the American Awareness of Africa
Washington D.C.
June 12, 1988

Doctor of Laws (Honouris Causa)
Bridgewater State College
Bridgewater, Massachusetts (May 23, 1987).

Albert Schweitzer Professor
State University of New York at Binghamton
Binghamton, NY (1989 to present).

Elected Fellow, African Academy of Sciences, Nairobi, Kenya
1989.

Member of Group of Eminent Persons on Black and African Reparations,
Organization of African Unity,
Addis Ababa (from 1992).

Distinguished Africanist Award
African Studies Association of the United States (1993).

Distinguished Service Award
National University of Lesotho
Maseru, Lesotho (1995).

Enstooled as "Prince among Writers" (Literary Nana)
By Pan-African Writers' Association, Accra, Ghana
1996.

Ibn Khaldun Professor-at-Large
Graduate School of Islamic and Social Sciences
Leesburg, Virginia (1996-2000).

Distinguished Global Cultural Humanist Award
New York African Studies Association
1997.

Icon of the 20th Century
Lincoln University, Pennsylvania (1998).

Marcus Garvey-W.E.B DuBois Award
Pan-African Unity
Morgan State University
Baltimore, Maryland (1998).

Walter Rodney Distinguished Professor
University of Guyana
Georgetown, Guyana (1998).

Fellow, Institute of Governance & Social Research
Jos, Nigeria (from 1998).

Chair, Center for the Study of Islam and Democracy
Washington, DC (1999 to present).

Harvard University McMillan-Stewart Lecturer
W.E.B Du Bois Institute (March 2000).

Doctor of Letters (Honouris Causa)
Nkumba University
Entebbe, Uganda (March 2000).

Doctor of Letters (Honouris Causa)
University of Ghana
Legon, Accra, Ghana.

"**On Literature and the Lords,**" tribute to Mazrui's works in the House of Lords, London (June 2000).

Founding Father, Project "One Hundred Greatest African Books of the Last One Hundred Years," Zimbabwe International Book Fair, Harare and Cape Town, 2000 to 2002.

Fellow, Third World Academy of Sciences (TWAS) Beirut, Lebanon, and Trieste, Italy (From 2002).

First Abdulsalami A. Abubakar Distinguished Lecturer
Chicago State University
Chicago, Illinois (February 23, 2001).

Award of Honorary Membership "in recognition of immense contribution to African Literature," Pan-African Writers Association (Headquarters: Accra, Ghana) (2001).

Elected as Africa's Cultural Messiah, W.E.B. DuBois Center in Pan-African cultures, Accra, Ghana (2001).

Chairman, The Development Policy Management Forum, Addis Ababa, Ethiopia, from 2001.

Member of Group of Eminent Personalities, appointed by Secretary General of the United Nations, to evaluate Africa's Development in the 1990s (2001-2002).

Appendix

Member of Panel of Eminent Personalities appointed by Secretary-General of the Organization of African Unity (OAU) to advise him on the transition from the O.A.U. to the African Union (2002).

Fellow, Third World Academy of Sciences (TWAS) Beirut, Lebanon, and Trieste, Italy (From 2002).

Awarded Doctor of Letters, Honoris Causa, by the University of Ghana, Legon, Accra, in March 2002.

Founding Father of Project of Africa's Best Books of the twentieth century, and official orator for the Award of the Literary Prize to former President Nelson Mandela for his book, **LONG MARCH TO FREEDOM**, Cape Town, South Africa, July 2002.

Barbara Ward Distinguished Lecturer, World Congress of the Society for International Development, Dar es Salaam, Tanzania, June 2002.

SELECT HONORIFIC PUBLICATIONS

THE GLOBAL AFRICAN: A Portrait of Ali A. Mazrui
Edited by Omari H. Kokole
Africa World Press, Trenton, NJ (1998).

THE MAZRUIANA COLLECTION
A Comprehensive Annotated Bibliography of the Published Works of Ali A. Mazrui
Edited by Abdul Samed Bemath
Sterling Publishers Private Limited, New Delhi, India
Africa World Press, Trenton, NJ (1998).

THE SCHOLAR BETWEEN THOUGHT AND EXPERIENCE
A Biographical Festschrift in Honor of Ali A. Mazrui
Edited by Parviz Morewedge
Global Publications, Binghamton, 2002..

Bibliography

Ahmed, A. (2002), 'Ibn Khaldun's Understanding of Civilizations and the Dilemmas of Islam and the West Today,' *Middle East Journal*, 56, 1, Winter, 1-26.

Ajami, F. (2001), 'The Sentry's Solitude,' *Foreign Affairs*, 80, 6, 2-16.

Alamin Mazrui (2001), 'The African Impact on American Higher Education: Ali Mazrui's Contribution', in P. Morewedge (ed.), *The Scholar between Thought and Experience: A Biographical Festschrift in Honor of Ali A. Mazrui*, Global Publications, Institute of Global Cultural Studies, 3-22.

Alegre, E. (1973), 'The Modernization of Japan and Its Limits' in Japan and The Japanese, Compiled by The Mainichi Newspapers, Tokyo & San Francisco, Japan Publications Inc., 110-129

Armour, C. (2000), Review of *The Mazruiana Collection: A Comprehensive Annotated Bibliography of the Published Works of Ali Mazrui, 1962-1997* by Abdul Samed Bemath, in the *Journal of Modern African Studies*, 2000, 716-717.

Assuon, B. (1982), Thoughts on the Significance of Meiji-Japan's Experience of Modern development for the Future Education in Ghana-Africa, Tokyo, IDE.

Benedict, R. (1993), *The Chrysanthemum and the Sword: Patterns of the Japanese Culture*, Tokyo, Charles E. Tuttle.

Bemath, A. S. (1998), *The Mazruiana Collection: A Comprehensive Annotated Bibliography of the Published Works of Ali A. Mazrui, 1962-1997*, Johannesburg: Foundation for Global Dialogue.

Braverman, A. (1994), *Warrior of the Zen: The Diamond-hard Wisdom mind of Suzuki Shosan*, New York, Tokyo, London, Kodansha International.

Brown, C. (1999), 'Susan Strange: A Critical Appreciation,' *Review of International Studies*, 25, 531-535.

Buchanan, W. and H. Cantril (1953), *How Nations See Each Other: A Study in Public Opinion*, Westport: Greenwood press.

Bull, Hedley (1978), *Times Literary Supplement*, December 1, 1978.

_____ . (1966), "International Theory: The Case for a Classical Approach," *World Politics*, 18, 3, 361-377.

Cox, R. W. (1992), 'Towards a Post-Hegemonic Conceptualization of

World Order: Reflections on the Relevancy of Ibn Khaldun,' in J. N. Rosenau and E. Czempiel (eds.), *Governance without Government: Order and Change in World Politics*, Cambridge, New York, Post Chester, Melbourne, Sydney: Cambridge University Press, 132-159.

Choy, L. (1995), *Japan: Between Myth and Reality*, Singapore, World Scientific.

Dale, P. (1986), *The Myth of Japanese Uniqueness*, London & Sydney, Croom Helm.

Davidian, Z. (1994), *Economic Disparity Among Nations : A Threat to Survival in a Globalized World*, Calcutta, Oxford University Press.

Doob, L. (1968), Review of *On Heroes and Uhuru Worship* by Ali

D. Santos, (1978), 'The Crises of Development Theory and the Problem of Dependence in Latin America', in H. Berstein (ed.), *Underdevelopment and Development*, Middlesex, Penguin. Mazrui, Mawazo (Kampala), June.

Doran, M. (2002), 'Somebody Else's Civil War,' *Foreign Affairs*, 81, 1, 22-24.

Emerson, R. (1967), Review of *Towards a Pax Africana* by Ali Mazrui,' *MAWAZO*, 1, 1, 1967.

Evera, S. V. (1997), *Guide to Methods for Students of Political Science*, Ithaca and London: Cornell University Press.

Enan, M. (1975), *Ibn Khaldun: His Life and Work*, Lahore: Kashmir Bazar.

Feldman, S. (2001), 'Intersecting and Contesting Positions: Post-colonialism, Feminism and World-Systems Theory,' *Review*, 24, 3, 343-371.

Forde, S. (1995), 'International Realism and the Science of Politics: Thucydides, Machiavelli, and Neorealism,' *International Studies Quarterly*, 39, 2, 141-160.

Friedman, T. (2000), *The Lexus and the Olive Tree: Understanding Globalization*, New York: Anchor Books.

Fukuyama, F. (1992), *The End of History and the Last Man*, London: Penguin Books.

Fukuyama, F. (1995), *Trust: The Social Virtues and the Creation of Prosperity*, London: Hamish Hamilton.

Goldgeier, J. and M. McFaul, 'A Tale of Two Worlds: Core and Periphery in the post-Cold War Era,' *International Organization*, 46, 2, 1992, 467-491.

Harbeson, J. (1998), 'Culture, Freedom and Power in Mazruiana,' in O. Kokole (ed.), *The Global African: A Portrait of Ali*

Mazrui, Trenton, NJ, Asmara: Africa World Press, Inc., 23-35.
Harrison, L. and S. Huntington (2000), (eds.), *Culture Matters: How Values Shape Human Progress*, New York, Basic Books.
Hobbes, T. (1991), *Leviathan*, edited by R. Tuck, Cambridge: Cambridge University Press.
Hoebe, J. A. (1973), 'Social Bases for Economic Growth', *Japan and The Japanese*, Compiled by The Mainichi Newspapers, Tokyo & San Francisco, Japan Publications Inc., 52-72.
Hoffman, S. (1959), 'International Relations: The Long Road to Theory,' *World Politics*, 11, 3, 346-377.
Holsti, K. J (1998), 'Scholarship in an Era of Anxiety: the Study of International Politics during the Cold War,' *Review of International Studies*, 24, 17-46.
Honna N. and B. Hoffer (1984), *An English Dictionary of Japanese Way of Thinking*, Tokyo, Yuhikaku.
Hopkins, T. and I. Wallerstein (1982), *World Systems Analysis: Theory and Methodology*, London, Sage.
Huer, J. (1990), *The Fallacies of Social Sciences. A Critique of the Natural Sciences Model of Social Analysis*, New York: Peter Lang.
Huntington, S. (1996), 'The West: Unique, Not Universal,' *Foreign Affairs*. 75, 28-46.
_____.(1993), 'The Clash of Civilizations?' *Foreign Affairs*, 72, 3, 22-49.
Ibn Khaldun (1967), *The Muqaddimmah: An Introduction to History*, trans. From Arabic by F. Rosenthal, ed., Princeton, N.J.: Princeton University Press.
Ikenburry, G. (2002), 'America's Imperial Ambition,' *Foreign Affairs*, 81, 5, 44-60.
Jackson, R. and G. Sorensen (1999), *Introduction to International Relations*, Oxford: Oxford University Press.
Jervis, R. (2002), 'An Interim Assesement of September 11: What Has Changed and What Has Not,' *Political Science Quarterly*, 117, 1, 37-54.
_____ . (1998), 'Realism in the Study of World Politics,' *International Organization*, 52, 4, 971-991.
Kalu, Kelechi A. (2001), 'Post-Cold War Realism, Liberal Internationalism, and the Third World,' *Journal of Asian and African Studies*, 36, 2, 225-236.
Kant, I. (1991), *Political Writings*, edited by H. Reiss, Cambridge: Cambridge University Press.

Keohane, R. and J. Nye (1977), *Power and Interdependence: World Politics in Transition*, Boston: Little, Brown.
Kokole, O. (1998a), 'Introduction,' in O. Kokole (ed.), *The Global African: A Portrait of Ali Mazrui*, Trenton, NJ and Asmara, Eritrea, Africa World Press, xxi-xxiii.
_____. (1998b), 'The Master Essayist,' in O. Kokole (ed.), *The Global African: A Portrait of Ali Mazrui*, Trenton, NJ and Asmara, Eritrea, Africa World Press, 3-22.
_____. (nd), 'Ali A. Mazrui', in B. Lindfors and R. sander (eds.), *Twentieth-Century Caribbean and Black African Writers*, Second Series, Detroit, London: Gale Research Inc., 82-88.
Kotkin, J. (1992), *Tribes: How Race, Religion and Identity Determines Success in the New Global Economy*, New York, Random House.
Landes, D. (2000), 'Culture Make Almost All the Difference', in L. Harrison and S. Huntington (eds.), *Culture Matters: How Values Shape Human Progress*, New York, basic Books, 2-13.
Lebow, R. N. (2001), 'Thucydides the Constructivist,' *American Political Science Review*, 95, 3, 547-569.
Lewellen, T. (1995), *Dependency and Development: An Introduction to Third world*, Westport, Bergin and Garvey.
Locke, John (1997), *An Essay Concerning Human Understanding*, Edited by R. Woolhouse, London: Penguin Books (First Published in 1689).
Low, D. A. (1972), Review of *Protest and Power in Black Africa* by Ali Mazrui in *African Affairs* (London), April.
Mannheim, K. (1960), *Ideology and Utopia: An Introduction to the Sociology of Knowledge*, London, Routledge, London.
Markakis, John, 'Resource Conflict in the Horn of Africa,' *African Affairs*, 97, 389.
Marshall, B. (1992), *Teaching the Postmodern: Fiction and Theory*, New York: New York: Routledge.
Mazrui, A. (1968). 'From Social Darwinism to Current Theories of Modernization: A Tradition of Analysis', *World Politics*, 21, 1, 1968, 69-83.
Mazrui, Alamin (2001), 'The African Impact on American Higher Education: Ali Mazrui's Contribution,' in Parviz Morewedge (ed.), *The Scholar between Thought and Experience. A Biographical Festschrift in Honor of Ali A. Mazrui*, New York, Global Publications, Binghamton, University, Institute of Global Cultural Studies, 3-22.

Mazrui, Alamin (1998), 'Mazruiana and Global Language: Euro-centrism and African Counter-Penetration,' O. Kokole (ed.), *The Global African: A Portrait of Ali Mazrui*, Trenton, NJ and Asmara, Eritrea, Africa World Press, 155-172.

Mazrui, Ali A. (2002a), 'Nkrumahism and the Triple Heritage in the Shadow of Globalization,' Aggrey-Fraser-Guggisberg Memorial Lectures (Draft), University of Legon, Accra, Ghana (Part I), pps. 8.

_____.(2002b), 'Nkrumahism and the Triple Heritage in the Shadow of Counter-Terrorism,' Aggrey-Fraser-Guggisberg Memorial Lectures (Draft), University of Legon, Accra, Ghana (Part II), pps. 15.

_____. (2002c), 'Nkrumahism and the Triple Heritage: Out of the Shadows,' Aggrey-Fraser-Guggisberg Memorial Lectures (Draft), University of Legon, Accra, Ghana (Part III), pps. 13.

_____. (2002d), 'Nigeria between Lord Lugard and the Digital Divide: Political Culture and the Skill Revolution,' africaresource.com. pps. 8.

_____. (2002e), 'From Structural Adjustment to the Sacred Adjustment: Globalization and the New Sectarian Politics in Africa,' Draft., Lecture Delivered at the World bank, Washington, D. C., and Sponsored by the World Bank Office of the Africa Publishing Initiative and the Africa Club of the World bank and the IMF, 2 April, pps. 28.

_____. (2002f), 'The Truth between Tyranny and Terror: The United States, Israel and Hegemonic Globalization,' Keynote Address at the 5th Conference of the International Center for Contemporary Middle Eastern Studies, Eastern Mediterranean University, Cyprus, 25-27 April, pps. 23.

_____. (2002g), *The Titan of Tanzania: Julius K. Nyerere's Legacy*, Institute of Global Cultural Studies, Global Publications, Binghamton University.

_____. (2001a), 'Globalization and the Future of Islamic Civilization,' Speech delivered at Westminster University, September 3, 1-4.

_____. (2001b), 'Nyerere and I,' *Voices*, November, at www.ijele.com/voi/mazrui.htm

_____. (2001c), 'Ideology and African Political Culture,' in T. Kiros (ed), *Explorations in African Political Thought*, New York, London: Routledge, 97-131.

_____. (2001d), 'Pretender to Universalism: Western Culture in a Globalizing Age', *Global Dialogue*, vol. 3, no. 1, 33-45.

_____. (2001e), "The Ethics of War and the Rhetoric of Politics: 'The West and the Rest,'" Paper presented on a panel in an international conference, sponsored by the International Public Relations Association, Berlin, Germany, 14-17, October, pps. 14.

_____. (2000a), 'Cultural Amnesia, Cultural Nostalgia and False memory: Africa's Identity Crisis Revisited,' *African Philosophy*, 31, 2, 87-98.

_____. (2000b), 'The African Renaissance: A Triple Legacy of Skills, Values and Gender,' see, http://www.africacentre.org.uk/renaissance.htm#Ali A. Mazrui

_____. (2000c), 'Pretender to Universalism: Western Culture in the Globalizing Age,' BBC World, http://www.bbc.co.uk/wordservice/people/features/world-lectures/mazrui-lect.shtml, 1-18.

_____. (2000d), Annual Mazrui Newsletter. No. 24.

_____. (2000e), 'Africa in the Shadow of Clash of Civilizations: From the Cold War of Ideology to the Cold War of Race,' A Public Lecture delivered at the Auditorium of the National Universities Commission, Abuja, Nigeria, 22 June, pps. 28.

_____. (2000f), 'Transnational Ethnicity and Subnational Religion in Africa's Political Experience,' in K. Goldmann, U. Hannerz and C. Westin (eds.), *Nationalism and Internationalism in the Post-Cold War Era*, London and New York: Routledge, 37-50.

_____. (1999), 'Identity Politics and the Nation-State Under Siege: Towards a Theory of Reverse Evolution,' *Social Dynamics*, 25, 2, 5-25.

_____. (1998a), 'The Black of Woman and the Problem of Gender: An African Perspective,' in O. Kokole (ed), *The Global African: A Portrait of Ali Mazrui*, Trenton, NJ and Asmara: Africa World Press.

_____. (1998b), 'Woman as Victim Woman as Victor: A feminist Dilemma,' in O. Kokole (ed), *The Global African: A Portrait of Ali Mazrui*, Trenton, NJ and Asmara: Africa World Press.

_____. (1998c), 'The Social Dimensions of Culture and Contemporary Expressions,' Speech at a Workshop on Culture in Sustainable Development. Investing in Cultural and Natural Endowement, Sponsored by the World Bank and Unesco, September 28-29.

_____. (1998d), 'Globalization, Islam, and the West:

Between Homogenization and Hegemonization,' *The American Journal of Islamic social Sciences*, 15, 3, 1-13.
_____. (1998e), 'Can Proliferation End the Nuclear Threat?' *Middle East Affairs Journal*, 4, 2, 5-11.
_____. (1997a), 'Islamic and Western Values,' *Foreign Affairs*, 76, 5, 118-132.
_____. (1997b), 'Liberia and Ethiopia as pan-African Symbols: Rise, Decline and Change,' *Liberian Studies Journal*, 22, 2, 192-198.
_____. (1996a), 'Africa in the Twenty-First Century: Problems and Prospects,' Institute of Governance and Social research Annual Distinguished Lecture, no. A76, Jos, Nigeria, pps. 24.
_____. (1996b), "'Progress': Illegitimate Child of Judeo-Christian Universalism and Western Ethnocentrism—A Third World Critique,'" in L. Marx and B. Mazlish (ed.), *Progress: Fact or Illusion?* AnnArbor, MI: The University of Michigan Press, 153-154.
_____. (1996c), 'The Frankenstein State and Uneven Sovereignty,' in D. L. Sheth and A. Nandy (eds.), *The MULTIVERSE of Democracy: Essays in Honor of Rajni Kothari* New Delhi, Thousand Oaks, Calif., London: Sage, 50-57.
_____. (1996d), 'Perspective: The Muse of Modernity and the Quest for Development,' in P. G. Altbach and A. M. Hassan (eds.), *The Muse of Modernity: Essays on Culture As Development in Africa*, Trenton, New Jersey, Asmara: Africa World Press, Inc.
_____. (1995a), 'The African State as a Political refugee: Institutional Collapse and Human Displacement,' *International Journal of Refugee Law*, 7, 21-36.
_____. (1995b), 'The 'Other' as the 'Self' Under Cultural Dependency: The Impact of the Postcolonial University,' in G. Brinker-Gabler (ed), *Encountering the Other(s)*, Albany: State University of New York Press, 333-362.
_____. (1995c), 'The African State as a Political Refugee,' in D. R. Smock and C. A. Crocker (eds), *African Conflict Resolution. The US Role in Peacemaking*, Washington, D.C.: United States Institute of Peace Press, 9-25.
_____. (1995d), 'The African State as a Political Refugee: Institutional Collapse and Human Displacement,' *International Journal of Refugee Law*, Special Issue,

7, 21-36.

———. (1995e), 'Unequal Interdependence: Towards A Theory of North-South Relations,' *The Journal of African Policy Studies*, 1, 1, 7-30.

———. (1995f). 'The Erosion of the State and the Decline of Race: Bismarck to Boutros; Othello to O. J. Simpson,' Inaugural Address for the Foundation for Global Dialogue, South African Association for the Promotion of International Co-operation, Johannesburg, South Africa, 1-28.

———. (1994a), 'The Blood of Experience: The Failed State and Political Collapse in Africa,' *World Policy Journal*, vol. 12, 28-34.

———. (1994b), 'Global Apartheid? Race and Religion in the New World Order,' in T. Ismael and J. Ismael (eds), *The Gulf War and the New World Order: International Relations of the Middle East*, Gainesville: University Press of Florida, 521-535.

———. (1993a), 'Human Obligation and Global Accountability: From the Impeachment of Warren Hastings to the Legacy of Nuremberg,' in R. Falk, R. Johansen and S. Kim eds. *The Constitutional Foundations of World Peace*, New York: State University of New York Press, 329-347.

———. (1993b), 'Islam and the End of History,' *The American Journal of Islamic Social Sciences*, 10, 4, 512-535.

———. (1993c), 'Crisis in Somalia,' Africa Notes, February, 3-5.

———. (1993d), 'The Black Intifadah: Religion and Rage at the Kenya Coast,' *Journal of Asian and African Studies*, 4, 2, 87-93.

———. (1992a), 'The Dual Memory: Genetic and Factual,' *Transition*, Issue 57, 134-146.

———. (1992b), 'Afrocentricity Versus Multiculturalism: A Dialectic in Search of a Synthesis,' Paper delivered at the UCLA, under the sponsorship of the James Coleman African Studies Center, 5 May 1993 pps. 9.

———. (1992c), 'AFRABIA: Africa and the Arabs in the New World Order', *UFAHAMU: Journal of the African Activist Association*, 20, 3, 51-62.

———. (1991), 'Dr. Schweitzer's Racism,' *Transition*, Issue no. 53, 96-102.

———. (1990a), 'Religious Alternatives in the Black Diaspora: From Malcolm X to the Ras Tafari,' *Caribbean*

Affairs, 3, 1, January-March 1990, 157-160.

_____. (1990b), 'Satanic Verses or a Satanic Novel? Moral Dilemmas of the Rushdie Affair,' *Third World Quarterly*, 12, 1, 116-139.

_____. (1990c), *Cultural Forces in World Politics*, Oxford: James Currey.

_____. (1989a), 'Growing Up in a Shrinking World: A Private Vantage Point,' in Joseph Kruzel and James Rosenau (eds.), *Journeys through World Politics: Autobiographical Reflections of Thirty-four Academic Travelers*, Lexington: Mass., and Toronto: Lexington Books.

_____. (1989b), 'The Political Culture of War and Nuclear Proliferation: A Third World Perspective,' in H. C. Dyer and L. Mangasarian (eds.), *The Study of International Relations: The State of the Art*. London: Macmillan, 155-171.

_____. (1987a), 'Superpower Ethics: A Third World Perspective,' *Ethics and International Affairs*, 1, 9-21.

_____. (1987b), 'The Makerere Conspiracy: A View from Within,' *Africa Events*, May, 58-62.

_____. (1987c), 'Africa's Triple heritage of Play: Reflections on the Gender Gap,' in W. J. Baker and J. A. Manger (eds.), *Sports in Africa: Essays in Social History*, New York, London: Africana Publishing Company, 217-228.

_____. (1986a), *The Africans: A Triple Heritage*, Boston and Toronto: Little Brown & Co.

_____. (1986b), 'Africa's Triple Heritage and I', *Africa Events*, July/August, 34-38.

_____. (1985a), 'Uncle Sam's Hearing Aid,' in S. J. Ungar (ed), *Estrangement: America and the World*, Oxford: Oxford University Press, 181-192.

_____. (1985b), 'The Third World and International Terrorism,' *Third World Quarterly*, 7, 2, 348-349.

_____. (1985c), 'Africa and the Search for a New International Technological Order', in P. Ndegwa, L. Mureiti and R. Green (eds.), *Development Options for Africa*, Nairobi, Oxford University Press, 177-185.

_____. (1985d), 'Africa between Ideology and Technology: Two Frustrated Forces of Change', in G. M. Carter and P. O'Meara (eds.), *African Independence: The First Twenty-Five Years*, Bloomington, Indiana University Press.

_____. (1984), 'Africa Entrapped: Between The Protestant Ethic and the Legacy of Westphalia,' in Hedley Bull and Adam

Watson (eds.), *The Expansion of International Society*, Oxford: Clarendon Press.

———(1984b), *Africa between the Meiji restoration And the Legacy of Ataturk: Comparative Dilemmas of Modernization*, Ankara: TISA Matabaacilik Sanayl Ltd.

———. (1983a), 'Africa: The Political Culture of Nationhood and the Political Economy of the State,' *Millenium: Journal of International Studies*, 12, 3, 201-210.

———. (1983b), 'Zionism and Apartheid: Strange Bedfellows or Natural Allies?' *Alternatives*, vol. ix, 73-97.

———. (1982a), *The Moving Cultural Frontier of World Order: From Monotheism to North-South Relations*, Working Paper No. 18, World Order Models Project, New York: Institute for World Order.

———. (1982b), 'The Computer Culture and Nuclear Power: Political Implications for Africa,' in T. Shaw (ed.), *Alternative Futures for Africa*, Boulder: Westview Press.

———. (1981a), 'Changing the Guards from Hindus to Muslims: Collective Third World Security in a Cultural Perspective,' *International Affairs*, 57, 1, 1-20.

———. (1981b), 'Exit Visa from the World System: Dilemmas of Cultural and Economic Disengagement,' *Third World Quarterly*, 3, 1, 62-76.

———. (1981c), 'Political Nostalgia,' *Ibadan Journal of Humanistic Studies*, 3, 2, 1-17.

———. (1980a), 'Technology, International Stratification, and the Politics of Growth,' *International Political Science Review*, 1, 1, 63-79.

———. (1980b), *The African Condition*, New York: Cambridge University Press.

———. (1980c) 'Military Rule and the Re-Africanization of Africa: Amin in Uganda,' (Co-author D. F. Gordon), in I. J. Mowoe (ed) *The Performance of Soldiers as Governors: African Politics and the African Military*, Washington, D. C., University Press of America, 414-464.

———. (1980d), 'Beyond Dependency in the Black World: Five Strategies for Decolonization,' in A. Yansane (ed.), *Decolonization and Dependency: Problems of Development of African Societies*, Westport, Connecticut, London: Greenwood Press.

———. (1979), 'Nationalist and Statesman: From Nkrumah

Bibliography

and De Gaulle to Nyere and Kissinger,' *Journal of African Studies*, 6, 4, 199-205.

_____. (1978a), *Political Values and the Educated Class in Africa*, Berkley and Los Angeles: University of California Press.

_____. (1978b), *The Barrel of the Gun and the Barrel of Oil in North-South Equation*, World Order Models Project, Working Paper No. 5, New York: Institute for World Order.

_____. (1977a), 'The Warrior Tradition and the Masculinity of War,' *Journal of Asian and African Studies* (Leiden), 12, 1-4, 69-81.

_____. (1977b), 'Soldiers as Traditionalizers: Military Rule and the Re-Africanizing of Africa,' *Journal of Asian and African Studies*, 12, 1-4, 236-258.

_____. (1977c). 'Boxer Muhammad Ali and Soldier Idi Amin As International Political Symbols: The Bioeconomics of Sport and War,' *Comparative Studies in Society and History*, 19, 1, 189-215.

_____. (1977d), *Africa's International Relations: The Diplomacy of Dependency and Change*, London, Ibadan, Nairobi: Henmann; Boulder, Colorado: Westview Press.

_____. (1977e), 'Gandhi, Marx and the Warrior Tradition,' *Journal of Asian and African Studies,* 12, 1-4, 179-196.

_____. (1976a), 'The Bolsheviks and the Bantu: from the October revolution to the Angolan Civil War,' *Survey*, 22, 3-4, 288-306.

_____. (1976b), 'Religious Strangers in Uganda: From Emin Pasha to Emin Dada,' *African Affairs*, 76, 302, 21-38.

_____. (1976c), 'The Baganda and the Japanese: Comparative Response to Modernization,' *Kenya Historical Review*, 4, 2, 167-186.

_____. (1976d), 'Kenneth Kaunda: From Satyargha to détente,' *African Social Research*, no. 22, December, 155-159.

_____. (1975a), 'World Culture and the Search for Human Consciousness,' in Saul H. Mendlovitz (ed.), *On the Creation of A Just World Order. Preferred World for the 1990's*, New York: The Free Press, pp. 1-37.

_____. (1975b), 'Academic Freedom in Africa: The Dual Tyranny,' *African Affairs*, 74, 297, 393-400.

_____. (1975c), 'Ecclecticism as an Ideological Alternative: An African Perspective,' *Alternative*, 1, 465-486.

_____. (1975d), *The Political Sociology of the English Language: An African Perspective*, The Hague: Mouton.

_____. (1974a), *World Culture and the Black Experience*, Seattle and London, University of Washington Press.

_____. (1974b), 'Piety and Puritanism Under a Military Theocracy: Uganda Soldiers as Apostolic Successors,' in C. M. Kelleher (ed.), *Political Military Systems: Comparative Perspectives*, Beverly Hills, London: Sage Publications, 105-124.

_____. (1973a), 'The Lumpen-Proleteriat and the Lumpen-Militariat: African Soldiers as a New Political Class,' *Political Studies*, 21, 1, 1-12.

_____. (1973b), 'The Making of an African Political Scientist,' *International Social Science Journal*, 25, 1-2, 101-116.

_____. (1973c), 'The Yellow Man's Burden? Race and Revolutions in Sino-African Relations,' in Ian Wilson (ed.), *China and the World Community*, Sydney: Angus and Robertson, 152-178.

_____. (1972), *Cultural Engineering and Nation-Building in East Africa*, Evanston, Ill., Northwestern University Press.

_____. (1971), *The Trial of Christopher Okigbo*, New York: The Third Press.

_____. (1970), 'Leadership in Africa: Obote of Uganda,' *International Journal*, vol. 25, no. 3, Summer, 538-564.

_____. (1969a), *Violence and Thought. Essays on Social Tensions in Africa*, London and Harlow, Longmans.

_____. (1969b), 'European Exploration and Africa's Self-Discovery,' *The Journal of Modern African Studies*, 7, 4, 661-6676.

_____. (1969c), 'Political Science and Political Futurology: Problems of Prediction,' *Proceedings of the University of East Africa Social Science Council Conference* held in Makerere University, Kampala, Uganda, 172-188.

_____. (1968a), 'Thoughts on Assassination in Africa,' *Political Science Quarterly*, 58, 40-58.

_____. (1968b), 'Political Superannuation and the Trans-class Man,' *International Journal of Comparative Sociology*, 9, 2, 81-96.

_____. (1968c), 'From Social Darwinism to Current Theories of Modernization. A Tradition of Analysis,' *World Politics*, 21, 69-83.

_____. (1967a), 'Islam, Political Leadership and Economic

Radicalism in Africa,' *Comparative Studies in Society and History*, 9, 3, 274-291.

———. (1967b), *On Heroes and Uhuru Worship*, Longmans: London.

———. (1967c), 'Tanzaphilia,' *Transition*, 6, 31, 20-31.

———. (1967d), *Towards a Pax Africana: A Study of Ideology and Ambition*, Chicago: Chicago University Press.

———. (1967e), *The Anglo-African Commonwealth: Political Friction and Cultural Fusion*, Oxford and New York: Pergamon Press.

———. (1964), 'The United Nations and Some African Political Attitudes', *International Organization*, 18, 3, 499-520.

———. (1963a), 'Edmund Burke and Reflections on the Revolution in the Congo,' *Comparative Studies in Society and History*, 5, 2, 121-133.

———. (1963b), 'On the Concept of 'We Are All Africans,'' *American Political Science Review*, 57, 1, (March), 88-97.

Mazrui, Ali and Alamin Mazrui (1998), *The Power of Babel: Language & Governance in the African Experience*, Oxford, James Currey.

Mazrui, Ali and Andrew White, 'Collective Martyrdom in Modern History: From the Mandigo to the Mandelas, *Caribbean Affairs*, 2, 180-193.

McGwire, M. (2002), 'Shifting the Paradigm,' *International Affairs*, 78, 1, 1-28.

McDougall, W. (2002), 'Editor's Column,' *Orbis: A Journal of World Affairs*, 46, 1, 1-9.

Morewedge, P. (1998), 'The Onyx Crescent: Ali A. Mazrui on the Islamic/Africa Axis,' in O. Kokole (ed), *The Global African. A Portrait of Ali Mazrui*, Trenton, NJ and Asmara: Africa World Press, 121-149.

Morishima, M. (1982), *Why Japan Succeeded Western Technology and the Japanese Ethos*, Cambridge, Cambridge University Press.

Mowoe, I. (2001), 'Ali A. Mazrui-'The Lawyer,'' in Parviz Morewedge (ed.), *The Scholar between Thought and Experience: A Biographical Festschrift in Honor of Ali A. Mazrui*, Binghamton, NY: Institute of Global Cultural Studies, Global Publications, Binghamton University, 145-155.

Nafziger, E. W. (1995), *Learning from the Japanese: Japan's Pre-war development and the Third World*, Armong, NY and London, M. E. Sharpe, 1995.

Nettl, J. (1968), 'The State as a Conceptual Variable,' World

Politics, 20, 4, 559-92.

Nietzsche, F. (1998), *Twilight of the Idols or How to Philosophize with a Hammer*, Trans by Duncan Large, Oxford, New York: Oxford University Press.

Nkrumah, K. (1957), *The Autobiography of Kwame Nkrumah*, Edinburgh, Thomas Nelson and Sons Ltd.

Nyang, S. (1981), *Ali A. Mazrui: The Man and His Works*, The Third World Monograph Series, Lawrenceville: Brunswick.

Nye, J, and W. Owens. (1996), 'America's Information Edge,' *Foreign Affairs*, 75, 2, 20-36.

Ohmae, K. (1982), *The Mind of the Strategist: The Art of the Japanese Business*, New York, McGraw-Hill, Inc.

Ore R. and M. Sako (1989), *How the Japanese Learn to Work*, London and New York, Routledge.

Orwell, G. (1981), *A Collection of Essays*, San Diego, New York, London: HBJ Publishers.

Oweye, J. (1992), *Japan's Policy in Africa*, Lewiston, Edwin Mellen.

Park, S. (1979), Review of *Africa's International Relations: The Diplomacy of Dependency and Change.* By Ali A. Mazrui, Boulder, Colo. Westview Press, in *American Political Science Review*, 73, 691-692.

Philpott, D. (2000), 'The Religious Root of Modern International Relations,' *World Politics*, 52, 2, 206-245.

Popper, K. (1968), *The Logic of Scientific Discovery*, New York: Harper & Row.

_____. (1990), *Unended Quest: An Intellectual Autobiography*, Open Court, Chicago and La Salle.

Porter, T. (1994), 'Postmodern Political Realism and International relations Theory's Third Debate,' in C. T. Sjolander and W. S. Cox (eds.), *Beyond Positivism: Critical Reflections on International Relations*, Boulder and London: Lynne Rienner.

Richardson, l. (1994), 'Writing: A Method of Inquiry,' in N. Denzin and Y. Lincoln (eds), *Handbook of Qualitative Research*, Thousand Oaks: Sage, 516-529.

Rosenau, J. N. (1990), *Turbulence in World Politics: A Theory of Change and Continuity*, New Jersey: Princeton University Press.

_____. (1995), 'Security in a Turbulent World,' *Current History, Journal of Contemporary World Affairs*, vol. 94, no. 592, 193-200.

Rosenau, J. N. and M. Durfee (1995), *Thinking Theory Thoroughly. Coherent Approaches to an Incoherent World*, Boulder, San Francisco, Oxford: Westview Press.

Rothstein, R. (1991), (ed.), *The Evolution of Theory in International Relations*, Columbia, University of South California Press.

Ruggie, J. (1998), 'What Makes the World Hang Together? Neo-utilitarianism and the Social Constructivist Challenge,' *International Organization*, 52, 4, 855-885.

Russel, B. (2001), *The Scientific Outlook.* First Published 1931, New York: Routledge.

Russett, B., J. Oneal and M. Cox (2000), 'Clash of Civilizations or Realism and Liberalism Déjà vu? Some Evidence,' *Journal of Peace Research*, 37, 5, 583-608.

Salem, A. (2001), 'The Islamic Heritage of Mazruiana,' in Parviz Morewedge (ed.), *The Scholar between Thought and Experience: A Biographical Festschrift in Honor of Ali A. Mazrui*, Binghamton, NY: Institute of Global Cultural Studies, Global Publications, Binghamton University, 63-101.

Sawere, C. (1998), 'The Multiple Mazrui: Scholar, Ideologue, Philosopher, Artist,' in O. Kokole (ed), *The Global African. A Portrait of Ali Mazrui*, Trenton, NJ and Asmara: Africa World Press, 269-289.

Schwartz, T. and K. Skinner (2002), 'The Myth of Democratic Peace,' *Orbis: A Journal of World Affairs*, 46, 1, 159-172.

Seifudein A. (2002), *Anarchy, Order and Power in World Politics: A Comparative Analysis*, Aldershot: Ashgate.

Shaw, T. (1978) Review of *A World Federation of Cultures: An African Perspective* by Ali Mazrui, *Canadian Journal of Political Science*, xi, 1, 1978.

Shichihei, Y. (1992), *The Spirit of Japanese Capitalism and Selected Essays*, Trans. By L. Riggs and T. Manabu, Lanham, Madison Books.

Smith, A. (1993), *An Inquiry into the Nature and Causes of the Wealth of Nations*, edited by K. Sutherland, Oxford, New York, Oxford University Press.

Sorensen, G. (1997), 'An Analysis of Contemporary Statehood: Consequences for Conflict and Cooperation,' *Review of International Studies*, 23, 253-269.

Strange, S. (1988), *States and Markets*, London: Pinter.

Takeo, K. (1983), *Japan and Western Civilizations: Essays on Comparative Culture*, Tokyo, The University of Tokyo Press.

Thurow, L. (1992), *Head to Head: The Coming Economic battle Among japan, Europe and America*, St. Leonards: Allen and Unwin.

Tipson, F. (1997), 'Culture-clashification: A Verse to Huntington's Curse,' *Foreign Affairs*, 76, 2, 166-169.

Tobin, J. (1992), *Re-Made in Japan: Everyday Life and Consumer Taste in a Changing Society*, New Haven, Yale University Press.

Ufumaka, A. (1994), 'Who is Afraid of Ali Mazrui?' *African Profiles International*, April/May, 55-57.

Waever, O. (1998), 'The Sociology of Not So International Discipiline: American and European Developments in International Relations,' *International Organization*, 52, 4, 687-727.

Waever, O. (1997), 'Figures of International Thought: Introducing Persons Instead of Paradigms,' in *The Future of International Relations: Masters in the Making*, London, and New York: Routledge, 1-37.

Wallerstein, I. (1993), 'World –System Versus World-Systems; A Critique', in A. G. Frank and B. Gills (eds.), *The World System: Five Hundred Years or Five Thousand?*, London, Routledge.

Wallerstein, I. (1991), *Unthinking Social Science: The Limits of Nineteenth Century Paradigms*, Cambridge, Polity.

Wallerstein, I. (1999), *The End of the World As We Know It: Social Science for the Twenty-First Century*, Minneapolis, London: University of Minnesota Press.

_____. (1995), *Unthinking Social Science: The Limits of Nineteenth Century Social Sciences,* Cambridge, Polity.

_____. (1991), *Unthinking Social Science: The Limits of Nineteenth Century Paradigms*, Cambridge, Polity.

Walt, S. (2002), 'Beyond bin Laden: Reshaping US Foreign Policy,' *International Security*, 26, 3, 56-78.

Waltz, K. (2000), 'Structural Realism after the Cold War,'

International Security, Summer, 25, 1, 5-41.

Waever, O. (1998), 'The Sociology of Not So International Discipiline: American and European Developments in International Relations,' *International Organization*, 52, 4, 687-727.

_____. (1997), 'Figures of International Thought: Introducing Persons Instead of Paradigms,' in *The Future of*

International Relations: Masters in the Making, London, and New York: Routledge, 1-37.

Weber, M. (1964), 'The Theory of Social and Economic Organization,' in T Parsons (ed), New York, Free Press.

_____. (1958), *The Protestant Ethic and the Spirit of Capitalism. The Relationships Between Religion and the Economic and Social Life in Modern Culture*, New York: Charles Scribner's Sons.

Wendt, A. (1999), *Social Theory of International Politics*, Cambridge: Cambridge University Press.

_____. (1995), "Constructing International Politics", *International Security*, 20, 1, 71-81.

_____. (1992), "Anarchy is What States Make of It: The Social Construction of Power Politics" *International Organization*, 46, 1992, 391-425.

Index

A

Absolute gains 36, 37
Active Instability 135, 153, 156
Afghanistan 102, 118, 121, 131-132
Afrabia 136
Afro-Saxons 136
Afrocentricity 53, 150, 166
Aggressive dependency 136, 171
Akbar 185
Al Azhar 182
Al Qaeda 102-103, 120, 123, 130
Alamin Mazrui 11
Algeria 33, 173
Amin, Idi 66, 157, 161, 182
Androgynization 137, 144, 173
Annan, Kofi 22, 106
Anti-Semitism 14-15
Anyaoku, Emeka 18
Approaches to political theory 6
Armour, Charles 18-19
Authoritative pan-socialism 137, 144

B

Baganda 91
Balanced dependency 137
Barnett, Donald 63
Benevolent racism 137, 139, 159
Benevolent recolonization 138
Benevolent sexism 138, 159
Benign colonization 138, 156, 158-159
Benign racism 137-139, 159

Bi-racial slavery 139, 161, 174
Bin Laden 101, 120, 123, 174, 176
Black Orientalism 139-140
Blair, Tony 122, 124
Bodin, Jean 7
Bolsheviks 67
Bosnia 24
Britain 45, 147, 149, 151, 154
Buganda 67
Bull, Hedley 11, 16
Burke, Edmund 5, 21
Bush, George 107, 119, 120

C

Cairo 71
Calculus-friendly culture 140
Carr 50
Carthage 42
China 49, 121, 137, 162
Clanocracy 140
Clash of civilizations 40-43, 100-102, 104-118, 121-124, 127-130, 146, 148-150, 153
Classical realism 12
Columbus 65
Communism 39
Comparative antithesis 5, 64
Comparative empirical performance 49
Comparative politics 1, 9, 17, 35
Complex interdependence 24
Comprehensive globalization 141, 145, 150, 155
Conflictual politics 24
Continental jurisdiction 141, 163
Cox, Robert W. 182-184
Creative eclecticism 13, 185
Crippled capitalism 141
Cultural amnesia 32

Cultural dependency 38, 69, 171
Cultural engineering 34, 142
Cultural nostalgia 32
Cultural paradigm 181
Cultural relativism 49, 142, 146, 152
Cultural retribalization 142
Cultural treason 140
Czar 65, 67, 72, 157

D

Dar al Harb 127
Dar al Islam 125, 127
Darwin 69
Dawood, N.J. 183
Deductivism 3, 4, 7, 20
Defensive fanaticism 143
Denationalization of 137, 143,173
Diamond, Larry 39
Diplomatic cold storage 144
Dissident pan-socialism 137, 144
Division of control 144-145
Doob, Leonard 59
Doran, Michael 120
Dual society 145, 164
Dual tyranny 145
Dualistic approach 24
Dunn, Kevin 22, 23

E

Eastern Europe 143-144, 149, 158, 160, 168
Eclecticism 10, 13, 185
Economic globalization 141, 145,150, 155
Ecumenical state 145,161, 167
Egypt 34, 159, 182, 183
Egypticism 30
Einfuhlung 4

Einstein, Albert 4, 69
Electoral democracy 39
Electronic theocracy 146
Emerson, Rupert 67
Empirical observation 4
Enan, M.A. 184
End of History 38, 47-50, 74, 104-105, 107-110, 114-115, 131
Enslaving phase 146, 149-150, 153
Epistemology 57
Evangelical exploration 146, 169
Evangelical exploration 146
Evocative writing 62
Exploitative exploration 146-147, 169

F

Factual memory 147, 148
False memory 32
Feminism 12
Feudo-imperial interdependence 24, 147, 160
Formal imperialism 147
Fractured nation-state 148
Frankenstein state 45,148, 183
Fukuyama, Francis 38, 48-49, 108-110

G

Game theory 36
Gandhi 67
Genetic memory 147-148
Geneva Convention 103
Genocidal Phase 146, 148, 150, 153
Ghadafi 182
Ghana 89, 157
Global Africa 148
Global apartheid 149
Global Pan-Africanism 149, 172-

Globalization 17, 38-40, 111, 141, 145, 150, 152-153, 155, 170
Gloriana 150, 166, 168
Graham 119
Greece 33
Gulf War 112

H

Harbeson, John 10-11
Hastings, Warren 65
Hatchett, John 15
Hegemonic globalization 149-150, 153, 170
Hegemonic homogenization 150, 152
Hegemonization 39, 150, 152
Historical relativism 49, 142, 146, 152
Hitler 65, 116, 159
Hobbes, Thomas 21, 126
Hoffman, Stanley 51
Holy Roman Empire 65, 158
Homogenization 150-152
Horizontal integration 152-153
Huer, Jon 17
Hume, David 21
Huntington, Samuel 40-43, 54, 100-101, 109-112, 115-117, 121-122, 124, 127-128

I

Ibn al-Khatib 185
Ibn Khaldun 126, 179-185
Illiberal democracy 39
Imminent Instability 135, 153, 156
Imperial 114, 150
Imperial phase 146, 149, 153
Imperial reconstitution 153-154
Imperial reincarnation 153-154

Implicative closing 73
India 121, 140
Indonesia 124, 158, 170
Inductivism 4, 7
Informal imperialism 147, 154
Informational globalization 141, 145, 155
Inoguchi, Takashi 14
Institutional liberalism 41
Integrated cleavage 48, 155
Intellectual acculturation 155
Inter-African recolonization 138, 156, 158
Interdependence liberalism 41
Intimidatory leader 156-157, 161-162
Iran 123, 154
Iraq 112, 121, 154
Itote, Waruhiu 63

J

Japan 65, 124, 127, 151, 154
Japanese "miracle" 78-80, 93
Jervis, Robert 53
Jihad 120
Johannesburg 71
Jordan 124
Judeo-Christian Universalism 50

K

Kant, Immanuel 125, 126, 127
Kariyuki, M. 63
Kenya 36, 144, 146, 182
Kenyatta, Jomo 63, 144
Khatami, Pres. 123
Kin-country syndrome 112
King Abdullah 124
Kipling, Rudyard 65
Kokole, Omari 1, 18, 65

Kuhn, Thomas 69
Kuwabara, Takeo 83, 93
Kuwait 112

L

Latent instability 135, 153, 156
Leader of reconciliation 156, 161, 163
Lenin 65, 67, 70, 157
Leninist Czar 72, 157
Leys, Colin 16
Liberal democracy 39, 108-110, 127
Liberalism 29, 41, 151
Livingstone 65
Locke, John 5, 21, 67
Logic of Reasoning 2-3, 70
Low, D.A. 60
Lumpen militariat 157

M

Machiavelli 10, 126
Macroretribalization 158
Malignant colonization 158
Malignant racism 137, 159
Malignant sexism 138, 139, 159
Mannheim, Karl 52
Martin Luther King 182
Martyrdom 140, 171
Martyrdom complex 159
Marx, Karl 67, 70, 116, 157, 172
Marxism 49, 116, 151, 157, 158
Masculinity 11
Mature interdependence 147, 160, 166
Mauritius 34
Mboya, Tom 63
MccGwire, Michael 102
Metaphor 41, 62, 67, 68, 69
Methodology 2, 3, 7, 49, 63
Microretribalization 158, 160

Middle East 112, 136, 139
Military Democracy 160
Military Theocracy 161
Mill, John Stuart 21
Mitchell, Lynn 120
Mobilization leader 156-157, 161
Moisi, Dominique 123
Montesquieu 7
Morganthau, Hans 10-11
Morrow, Lance 120
Multiracial slavery 139, 161, 174
Murphy, Craig 22-23

N

NATO 119
Naturalistic 30
Neoclassical 30
Neoliberal institutionalism 12
Neorealism 12, 183
Nettl, J.P. 44
Neumann, Von 36
Nietzsche 30
Njama, Karari 63
Nkrumah, Kwame 63, 65, 67, 72, 157, 164
Non-normative social science 52
Normative social science 51, 52, 53
North Korea 23, 121
Nuclear Apartheid 12, 162
Nuremberg Trials 65
Nye, Joseph 10, 46, 47
Nyerere, Julius 137-138, 164, 182

O

Obote, Pres. Milton 58, 157
Okigbo, Christopher 36
Ontological 1, 36
Othello 65

P

Pan-pigmentationalism 162
Paradigm shift 59, 102,104
Patriarchal leader 156-157, 161-162
Pax-Africana 163
Pax-humana 163
Pearl Harbor 106
Perpetual peace 109, 126
Pfaff, William 116, 117
Pigmentational self-determination 164
Plural society 145, 164
Political assassinations 7
Political hygiene 164
Political legitimacy 2
Political nostalgia 165, 168
Political re-traditionalization 165
Political superannuation 164-165
Popper, Karl 4
Porter, Tony 32
Positivism 51, 61
Postmodern terrorism 100, 102-103,
Postmodernism 31, 32, 180
Postmodernist social constructivism 30-31
Primitive interdependence 24, 160, 165
Primordial socialism 166, 168
Progress 50, 106, 118-119
Public policy 101

R

Racial sovereignty 166-167
Re-sacrilizing of the state 144, 167, 173
Realism 11, 12, 24, 29
Reciprocal dependence 40
Reflection 3, 5
Reflexive predictions 113

Regime of truth 25, 31, 34, 100
Reincarnation 154
Relative gains 36-37
Religious nation 146, 167
Religious state 146, 167
Restorative nostalgia 168
Retarded socialism 168
Revolutionary socialism 166, 168
Rhythmic variation 65, 69, 71
Richardson, Laurel 62
Romantic gloriana 168, 169
Romantic primitivism 169
Rome 42
Roosevelt, Franklin D. 70
Rosenau, Pauline 32, 38, 109, 128
Ruggie, John 30
Russell, Bertrand 20
Rwanda 24, 35, 43

S

Sacred Suicide 74, 169
Salim 22
Sawere, Chaly 57
Schroeder 122, 123
Schweitzer, Albert 65
Scientific exploration 146-147, 169
Secular theocracy 100-102
Security dilemma 37
Semi-autobiographical 61-64, 74
Senghor, Sedar 182
Shaw, George Bernard 71
Simpson, O.J. 65
Sins of commission 170
Sins of submission 170
Skill revolution 38, 109, 129
Smith, Adam 82, 83
Social constructivism 29-31, 33, 50, 53, 180

Social mobility 37
Socio-historic 6
Socrates 30
Soft power 46, 47
Somalia 24, 35, 43, 140
Sorensen, George 23
Soviet Union 35, 39, 49, 108, 137, 143
State collapse 43
Statistical analysis 20
Strange, Susan 45-46
Structural dependency 142, 170
Structures of power 45-46
Styles of argument 63
Sub-Saharan Pan-Africanism 171, 175
Submissive dependency 136, 171
Submissive fatalism 143, 171
Submissive martyrdom 171
Suzuki, Shosan 83

T

Taliban 103, 119, 120, 170
Tanzaphilia 172
Techno-cultural gap 172
Theory of Convergence 40
Theory of Knowledge 5
Theory of Reverse Evolution 70, 172
Third World 16, 46, 106
Thucydides 30, 180
Tipson, F. S. 117
Toynbee, Arnold 184
Trans-Atlantic Pan-Africanism 173
Trans-class man 173
Trans-Saharan Pan-Africanism 173, 175
Tribal conservatism 174
Tribalism 24, 35
Triple Heritage 16, 34, 174
Turner, James 15

U

Uganda 34, 58, 65, 138, 157, 161, 173, 182
Uhuru worship 174
UN 22, 42, 119, 122, 138, 154
Uniracial slavery 139, 161
Unitary approach 6
Usamaphilia 174
Usamaphobia 174

V

Vedrine, Hubert 122
Vertical (Nuclear) Proliferation 175

W

Waever, Ole 14
Waltz, Kenneth 10
Weber, Max 44-45
Wells, H.G. 42
Wendt, Alexander 36, 130
West-Hemispheric Pan-Africanism 175
Western ethnocentrism 50
World-systems approach 12

Y

Yemen 34
Yugoslavia 24, 35, 43, 143, 149

Z

Zanzibar 2, 138, 155-156
Zionism 14-15, 159